CW00538892

Broken Sleep Anthologies

Broken Sleep Books 2018

Broken Sleep Books 2019

Broken Sleep Books 2020

Crossing Lines: an anthology of immigrant poetry

Hit Points: an anthology of video game poetry

Snackbox: Selected Legitimate Snacks, seasons 1 & 2

Broken Sleep Books 2021

ed. Kent & Baylis

Broken Sleep Books acknowledges the generous funding provided by Books Council of Wales to aid the publication of this book.

CYNGOR LLYFRAU CYMRU
BOOKS COUNCIL of WALES

ISBN: 978-1-915079-95-4

The authors have asserted their right to be identified as the authors of these Works in accordance with the Copyright, Designs and Patents Act 1988

Cover designed by Aaron Kent

Edited and typeset by Aaron Kent

Broken Sleep Books Ltd
Rhydwen,
Talgarreg,
SA44 4HB
Wales

Contents

PROSE

2021

Edited by:
Aaron Kent
&
Charlie Baylis

POETRY

A Light Worker

31/01/2021

Lucy Harvest Clarke

O Comely O Domestic

Down in the deep of the land cape
O comely O domestic

Down at the depth met zero
Keep on just wept horizon
My heart would not stop what's left

Deeper yet in serried conception
The thin in-let cosmic verse
Unpicked and strewn
What I could do not to you

And the water moon producing

Lower to the depths of certainty
Lowered reaching under so much to do
Stacked up in mood gravities
Yo peel the morn yo don't my turn
And please say sorrel

Here comes the lowly rattle
Read shake your heart treads

Patterns of the unlit
Where you are you so careful

Fires at the border crossing

Peachy here comes the base train
Follow the rooky down

Deep down the broken trail
My love so crassly done

The chicken snaps like a wish
The valley with any old rumble

Your ruckus of a crave to
Tell the rising
Enter at the finger bones

Please someone charity the elbow
At the shoulder

December

December you have covered it all and cancelled the rest.

December I can see - when I exhale - you erase.

December white triangle rinsed on pink horizon.

December a type of peak.

You exist but you were also made, isn't that right December.

Something came out of the sky, it was black and cold, and we named it December.

With your white shadow you remain ostensibly futile.

But it was December that knocked on your grandmother's door.

December it is land now covered in chalk.

The birds of December hang from branches, still warm.

December settles on gravel as an interface and we simply cannot ignore you.

December I think you illuminate contrast.

With your contrasting sides December, I sense blood.

December put the year down the hole.

Despite an effort given December can never be tabloid.

Flat December like two hundred and twenty two.

For this cavernous back wall I thank you December.

December I always have you under the stairs.

December the cold creeper, you mongrel - you have proved yourself rigid all right!

In the courtyard the walls are drying now, trying to picture December.

I did my best not to own you December but you made it so very easy.

December your sugary crisp is stuck in my spine.

I think you were once in love, weren't you, December.

It's like you decided December.

December rolled up to the knee, allowing for a dip.

The wind is December - a jostle and a wrestle - so marvellously tender.

Tender December, blindfolded throwing butter knives.

December I beg you give me back my letters.

Oh dear December, what is it you want from me?

Your dark dark night December, your dark dark night.

December - black solstice black dog.

Please I need December to leave me.

You and your screaming trees December covering the skeleton.

The lead in a boot December.

December like a crooked gate.

Climb over it but you just get to – December.

December a bit wanton like a promise or a risk.

But do you end it, December?

December – the star that cut the left index.

So December curt and controlling.

In earnest December at each man equally.

With your way of sticking to the centre December.
And when he came it was December and morning.

All across the panels in a milky courtyard they couldn't quite
put their finger on December.

Just the same as everything.

In this way you have to be December.

I remember the white walls.

Can't you cuddle up any other time.

December you have no opposite any more and no allies to
speak of.

December you gave her real blue lashes.

I don't feel that caustic word December - I live for you now.
People know you are cleanish December.

Something in the glass made an epigram, and they named it
December.

December likes touching my reading books.

Just a touch December.

For Mary, Marie, Maria,
After the Nectar, Pyre and Linden Tree

31/01/2021

Lucy Rose Cunningham

I

Mary, at 4 today

I carried more than the weight of my backpack
and the lady told me it was okay
but not what she expected,

not what I expected
as I ate breakfast ate miles
ate the last slot from
the same day appointments,

not what I expected
when the room ate my air ate my words
when the test ate my sensibility
the lady ate my stomach with
her bare hands and pressed

at 4 today

the holding clinging craving

intimacy taking place
inside,
the trouble
between us,

the individual silence of each finger padding
deriding the end of this
tender excess,

at 4 today.

***

Please hold.

***

Nectar envelops

the situation

            is getting warmer sweeter

                         heavier,

she found it
there, wrapped in jelly scented curtains
pale yellow ceiling to floor,
pale yellow potpourri, warm scented

nectar is a sticky cradle,
rocking 8 weeks of lethargic lullaby
lulling longing looping back
to a night of presence,

                now

              sticky warmth
               draining to

                            absence, stuck.

***

Please hold.

***

She liked its fragrance.

The gods liked sweetness
to keep their souls
tender,

sweetness saw
Aphrodite cleanse in nectar
Aphrodite put nectar in your words,
put nectar in my

womb,
her wild warmth held
tight, we clung
tight I cling
to my weight,
now clawed
shedding paper stack
tissue giving way to

red
mouths open
red pulsing to brown to

black
        is night in bedded frenzy,
                the Thames in hushed dusk,
                the emptiness when she stares at

the ceiling
4 hours into the new day,
4 tablets lining her gums,
4 hours of clotting red

sweetness,
saw Aphrodite cleanse in nectar,
put nectar in his words,
nectar in her womb.

***

Hold.

***

Basin cloud.

Ribbon clouds lace deep pink
over cranes outside,
floating in the upper part of the window,
small enough to hold in my palm.

Ribbon clouds lace deep pink in the basin,
bleeding sighs whispering across the tiles.

***

Imbibing,

drops slip between legs
the way peaches slide down throat;
honeyed sticking a reminder of aroused clinging,
in the neck of a duvet swallowing
two bodies' touch.

***

I tried calling, so I wrote instead.

***

{ For Ingeborg Bachmann }
Smoking blue

ignited slowly,

her bedcover,
the haze of
sleeplessness,

lit as she sensed blue warming to red to
white, the colour of

cotton fields to bed in   - growing tall

the flame when she caught
- seeing him leave

her hospital ceilings
from a moving trolley
- to grow or give in

to smoking ceilings inhaling bodies exhaling
cotton, to throw over her as she lay,

blue.

***

M-
she's learning to unlove
the deep blue took to be one's own.

***

Of Hearts

31/01/2021

Karen Dennison

At Point Nemo

At the height of youth, I circled earth.
It spun at my feet, a distant beauty;
admirers attracted into graveyard orbits.

For me the sun was another star
and though I learnt its physics,
I worshipped it as Ra, studied its secrets.

I was unbreakable and made of light
and time was for other people. I witnessed
the fall of *peace* - Mir breaking up

on re-entry with smoking hands and fireball-
fingertips, crashing into the South Pacific.
My own descent into waves was sudden,

knocked off course by junk and debris.
For decades I lay on the seabed
with other wrecks and remnants of life.

Diving down through miles of water,
you swam into the sunken city of my heart,
emptied my drowned mouth. I listened

to your stories of the surface, began to believe
in rebirth, in escaping gravity's grip on my bones;
felt like I was back in high orbit. But you left

how you arrived — a lone explorer on a mission,
fearless. And every night is terminal velocity,
nothing but the cemetery to break my fall.

***

*"Point Nemo" (oceanic pole of inaccessibility) is the area of ocean
furthest from land and is the location of the so-called Spacecraft
Cemetery where retired spacecraft are sent.*

Between the lines

White spaces are ghosted words
where I lifted my pen,
unwrote sorrow's wrist,

sewed up my lips. In the gaps,
my quiet hands unravel the sky
of that summer, stretch it

over the miles earth has spun
between now and then, throw dust
in my eyes. Pale skin lies across

the page; letters fallen from creased
palms anchor themselves in my heart.
My empty lines, scarred with loss,

pick at invisible seams, unstitch
the darkness I've been holding in.

The Impossible Museum

Enter the dome-roofed room
full of still-born words,
a universe of every unvoiced thought.

Pick up headphones and hear
the never-still brain whirr, watch on repeat
the broken images of dreams.

Peer through a chest-high cabinet of glass,
as wide as outstretched arms,
that holds a day's worth of exhaled breath.

Draw aside black curtains to witness
a love that ricochets in the cave of a skull,
never sees the light of day.

In the gift shop, purchase a vial of grief.
Drink it, if you dare, to feel it rattle
the prison door of another's ribs.

Moon song

At night she's a lidless eye watching our dreams
projected onto windows, walls. She enters
our arenas of fear, of large and small spaces,
immeasurable heights and falling.

She knows the destitute, the homeless, feels
their dust-cold shivers in her empty seas, drips
her thought-tears on midnight, all-night, drunks;
sings with them their songs, silently, silverly.

She longs for foxes to shadow her rocks; stuttering moths
and shape-shifting bats to shelter in her craters.
Sometimes she sees her face drowning in water,
as if contorted in a circus mirror.

It's then she catches sight of the blackness at her back
she's slowly falling into. And she knows what it means
to die, to grieve for earth's dark beating heart.

Immanence

Nothing right now is louder than rain
as if all the pebbles from Brighton Beach
have catapulted from the sky, each one
hitting the bullseye of a thought;

each thought like a fragile glass, each rim
circled by a licked finger, waves resonating
into one repeating wordless sound.

Under its weight, leaves mouth their hymn
struck by stony drops, hold out tongues
in communion. And as the seed of a blackbird's prayer
begins to grow it's snatched by a river cascading

down the roof of the house, diving from its gutters.
My reflection wavers from a watery other-world,
submerged, unreal; signals like a deep sea diver.

Writing the Camp

28/02/2021

Yousif M. Qasmiyeh

In arrival, feet flutter like dying birds

We think, sometimes,
That they came from countless directions,
From dim-coloured borders,
From the raging fire that devoured them in the beginning,
From absence.
Here they come again, so invite them over to our death.

The refugee is the revenant of the face.

O refugee, feast upon the other to eat yourself.

In arrival, feet flutter like dying birds.

In the camp, time died so it could return home.

Writing the camp

What makes a camp a camp? And what is the beginning of a camp if there is any? And do camps exist in order to die or exist forever?

Baddawi is my home camp, a small camp compared to other Palestinian camps in Lebanon. For many residents, it comprises two subcamps: the lower and the upper camps that converge at the old cemetery. As I was growing up, it was common for children to know their midwife. Ours, perhaps one of only two in the entire camp, was an elderly woman, who died tragically when a wall collapsed on top of her fragile body during a stormy day in the camp. The midwife was the woman who cut our umbilical cords and washed us for the first time. She lived by the main mosque – *Masjid al-Quds* – that overlooked the cemetery. She would always wait by the cemetery to stop those who she delivered on the way to school, to give them a kiss and remind them that she was the one who made them.

The camp is never the same albeit with roughly the same area. New faces, new dialects, narrower alleys, newly-constructed and ever-expanding thresholds and doorsteps, intertwined clothing lines and electrical cables, well-shielded balconies, little oxygen and impenetrable silences are all amassed in this space. The shibboleth has never been clearer and more poignant than it is now.

Refugees ask other refugees, who are we to come to you and who are you to come to us? Nobody answers. Palestinians, Syrians, Iraqis, Kurds share the camp, the same-different camp, the camp of a camp. They have all come to re-originate the beginning with their own hands and feet.

Now, in the camp, there are more mosques, more houses of God, while people continue to come and go, like the calls to prayer emanating at slightly varied times from all these mosques, supplementing, interrupting, transmuting, and augmenting the voice and the noise simultaneously.

Baddawi is a camp that lives and dies in our sight. It is destined to remain, not necessarily as itself, so long as time continues to be killed in its corners.

The camp is time

Who writes the camp and what is it that ought to be written in a time where the plurality of lives has traversed the place itself to become its own time.

How will the camp stare at itself in the coming time, look itself in the eye; the eye of time, the coming that is continually pending, but with a face — human or otherwise — that is defaced? The camp is a time more than it is a place. Upon and above its curves, time remembers its lapses to the extent that it is its time — the one whose time is one — that preys on a body that is yet to be born.

In crucifying time neither it nor we can recognise the crucified.

God, incinerate the camp save the dialect. God, incinerate the camp, save the dialect.

The incinerator of time is the camp.

What is it that makes a sight worth a sighting when the seer can use his eyes alone for an enormity that no eyes can actually see? Is it the camp or is it its time that should be returned to its body to reclaim its body as a dead thing with multiple previous lives and none.

I write for it knowing that this is the last time that I write for it, herein the time is last and the last, it may belong to a no-beginning-no-end, but what it definitely has is its camp. The camp is time and time is the camp.

The possessive is what possesses the guilt that transcends all guilt and yet co-exists with itself until it becomes an event in its own guilt. But is it, is it my camp?

What am I saying right now, in this specific instant and under the false impression that the camp is mine? I say that it is the autobiography of the camp that is autobiographising the camp, suspended in time it is, while we deliberate the impossibility of narration in that context. In order to think of narration, not necessarily its narration, we follow it discreetly in the shape of ash.

In time, the mask takes off its mask.

The foot that treads is also time.

In time, we impregnate time with its time.

Time gives birth to nothing. The nothing that is raging nearby is our only time.

Time, tell us where your private parts are?

In the camp, time is hung like threads of dried okra.

It is a camp despite the name

Existence, as it is, happens in the intentions of things.

A sign or signs piled on top of one another, barely separated by air and the narrowest of voids: white on blue or blue on white. There is a background – an undercoat – and then the words. But which is which? On the sign are arrows pointing to places, including to Baddawi camp. Names of old and new places neatly and orderly enclosed in this rectangular space. Positioned then adjusted to be made more visible to passersby and cars alike.

It is the Baddawi slope. The road that leads to everywhere and nowhere. The exact road which gave us and my mother trepidations as she stopped taxis on the main road going to Nahr Al-Bared camp. We would, upon my mother's prodding, hide behind her. Most of the time seven little bodies clutching her dress, looking for a handful of cloth, most of the time ending up inadvertently clutching each others' hands. The taxi driver would normally drive off the moment my mother would start asking him for a discounted fee: 'They are little, treat them as one. All of them on one seat and myself on another.'

My mother, to secure a ride that does not go beyond our limited financial means, would contract us into one: one body made of seven heads like a mythical creature who only grows in the camp. Many self-subtracted to one.

The sign is new or at least it previously was not there. The first sign to point to "Baddawi camp" alongside other places. The first sign to have the word 'camp' within its folds – a piece of evidence to the existence of the camp. To the presence of a place whose name is validated by a correspondence, a genitive one, between the proper 'Baddawi' and the noun 'camp' and yet it is the latter which is always remembered. It is a camp despite the name.

Confessions

He alone could scribble something so obscure in my school
report. I would look, eyes wide, at shapes as textured as the
palm of his hands. Elongated things, criss-crossed roads,
intentional or semi-intentional smudges, bruises, faint or
otherwise, around, above, through and underneath his name,
Mustafa; the chosen, the prophet, or just the name of someone
who happened to know how to drag a pen across a small box, a
space slightly bigger than a keyhole, usually a blue *Bic*, always
counterfeit from the corner shop in my camp.

My mother would have her fingerprints taken at the gate of
the UNRWA Distribution Centre, always in the company of a
headscarf, wrinkly like the camp's chapped sky. I would say: Let
me do it for you, to show you how a signature is born. A neat
signature like that woman's lipstick, across the aisle, the one
who only comes to us like a season at the end of the month. Or
let me tell you a secret: my copying my father's signature, with
a different name, a different time, in my friend's report pre-
tending to be the father. The father who shot the three-legged
stray dog in the head on a whim. I grafted my father's lines into
whiteness, once, twice, ten times, until we both shouted: This
almost looks like a
signature.

The rations would be dragged from one end to another in a
wheelbarrow. Flour, tins of tomato paste and corned beef, the
occasional sardines, lentils, vegetable oil and ghee. Not pushed
by me but by our neighbour's son, inked arms and shoulders,
with illegible names and shapes, who would
always pray in the last row to leave the mosque first to sell his
rotting vegetables and what he steals from the rations
to the outcoming worshippers. A trace of flour the
wheelbarrow would leave from the Centre to the house – an
amount, as my mother would say, that amounts to a day's
worth of silent mouths.

Confession

To confess
to arrive in the past at God's doorstep
to know what was said, with a script's precision still lying on the tongue
to sign the past as a pact between God
and God

My Grandfather

Hallucinations or fallen olives and shadows
in once furrowed furrows
now transient dreams
Elapsed blossoms awaiting old footsteps
The omen of the few

Fragile is the language

The fragile field
The fragile ears of corn
The fragile eye
A wilting flower on a ruin
A summer and another summer that escaped time

A fragile heart
The fragile language

American Ingénue

28/02/2021

Cathleen Allyn Conway

Prologue: Disappear Here

Today I strangled my twin sister—
not a pleasant way to wake up.

She is the distraction I needed:
her chalky face, her purple-lined

mouth; her chopstick legs and bony
knees and a head like someone stuck

a pumpkin on a neck.
I loved her in dreams,

blah-coloured eyes and hair
a dull yellow mess of split ends.

Her throat tightened,
my throat tightened,

and I faced the skyline. Reached
again into my bag of sorrows.

This is how life presents itself in New York,
maybe anywhere, at the end of the century:

LIZ THAN ZERO (2)
I drive to Todd's house,
but he isn't there

and so I sit in his room
and put a movie in the Betamax

and call Steven
and ask him if nuts are sensitive to cracks

and does it matter
and he says, 'turn sideways and stick out your tongue; you could
pass for a zipper'

and I draw on a piece of paper that's next to the phone
and he says 'aren't you lucky to have a nice daddy'

and it was obviously a dismissal
and he says, 'I'm going to have trouble squeezing my head out the
door'

and I say 'I know'
and there's a long silence heavy with irony before he says 'okay'

and I say 'our blankets are besieged by boys'
and hang up.

SIGHTSEEING

I want to see him bleed.

I want to see blood bubble out his nose

I want to see him tied up with wire; his mouth, his face, his balls, all duct-taped

I want him to scream when I push

I want him to hear that I hate him, that he's the most awful person I've ever met

I want him to know New York doesn't compare to a new pair of culottes

I want to see him look like Prince Charming

I want him to hand me a glass, to kiss me

I want to see he has more in mind than kissing

I want him to slap my arms to the couch

I want his mouth on my throat

I want to see the lights blaze at my hostess's apartment

I want her to see I am gloved in her daughter's dress

but it is dark and chilly and the ride through Central Park isn't fun anymore.

TAXI DRIVER

This is all her fault:

Stuck in a gridlocked cab heading downtown,
the driver knocks on the plexiglass divider.

His smile is impenetrable. I put the Walkman
back on, but he motions to me.

My mouth tastes funny, like a croak throbbed up
from the pit of my stomach in drunk hiccups.

There's a long pause while he stares at me;
grim smile fading in the rearview mirror.

I see the locks lower in a flash,
hear the hollow clicking noise.

THIS IS NOT AN EXIT

I'm getting sick. I am plastic.
There could be a telethon for
all the things wrong with me.
This is what we do to flee ourselves.
It's easier than being happy.

My mother cleaned out my closet.
This is what we do to please others.
She has her own sense of order;
you never know when her wicked gleam
will stare you into a tiny, shrinking smudge.

Everything was veiled while I was gone.
All night, stood here, a depressed pile
of notebooks floating two feet off
the pavement, another broken scene
in what passes for my life, my past
spelled out in toilet paper on the lawn.

The Dolphin House

28/02/2021

Richard O'Brien

You & me & the incredibly distant island universes

The man behind the glass removes his gloves.
The man without his gloves, glittered in salt,
flips up his goggle glasses, and he looks
like a woodsman training as a legal clerk,
tucked tightly in his suit — savage and tall.
His pockets brim with pens. His notes are damp.
He cracks the door.
             You want to speak to me?

When John drinks coffee, and he does drink coffee,
it's squid-ink black and his jitter's justified.
That's how we do it in St. Paul, he says,
but tell me about you.
                              I tried.
I tried to hold my threadbare quilt of life —
some college, and a few hostessing shifts —
up to him, and he burnt through and charged on.
He told me that he was a journalist.
No, that's not right, he said. A generalist,
which seemed concerned with keeping people sane,
although of course (he said) so few of us are.

Stubs in the ashtray. Grey mulch in the cup.

If you could see into my soul, John said,
assuming that you think the soul exists,
what would you see?
                      I didn't know.

He told me, and it was a litany:
the miles from Como to Cathedral Hill;
the baseball stats for 1934;
the fields of science and psychology,

all overlapping like a magic eye;
the words of Christ, of Huxley and Karl Marx,
and how it felt to drive a well-built car,
guide in your hand a finely-made machine;
genetics as a branch of moral law,
and fucking as epistemology —

he used that word. Epistemology.
Asked me to wait for him to finish work.

I hold the joint like a laser
scanning the surface of the moon.
John bathes in thought, while I just

slowly

pulse

and what he says is *Margaret, your mind —*
with all its files and drawers, all its dark rot —
has barely opened up onto itself.
You're still so young. I like it that you're young,
but how — and tell me this — how can we hope
to know, to truly know, the dolphin's mind
when all we understand about ourselves
is echoes, ego — a rat stuck in a tube
never suspecting life whirls on outside —
when we so feebly sound our own still depths,
how can we reach another consciousness?

The mirror in the car is all his eyes.

I didn't know. I said I didn't know.

Grand mal

That dolphin diddled itself to death, John said,
eyes glazed — Marineland, 1957.
They'd drilled a steel sleeve into its head
and let it push the lever with its beak
to trigger — whistles, barks, Bronx cheers; a jammed switch.
Then blasts of airborne phonemes. Bounced from heaven,
its killing lack had stunned him into speech,
like pleasure was the origin of language.

That's how it was when John was called to science.
Alone on the farm with his father's exercise belt,
aged ten, he buckled into the appliance.
Waves of the purest bliss he'd ever felt:
Godlike vibrations. Shamed, he swore: *The truth
is wider than any damned confession booth.*

Everyone loves to talk to a baby

A ball, a Ba Bee block, a bobo clown.
A burst of sound.
Tell me your name —
all things should have a name.

A learn, a lapse.
Bring ball, turn tail
for tummy rubs.
A broom to ward him off during my meal.

Colour is tough, understandably.
We spend the morning greeting,
you & me — *hello, hello*!
The schedule says: *Relax,* and so we do.

B-b-b-b-b-b-b-b-b-brush!
Demands and diamonds.
Soon I'll find a way
of siphoning the milky water clean.

A very precious sort of thing

audible "pop."
extrusion from
the genital groove.
penis rubbing,
fully erect, on leg.
perineal stimulation
offered, to subjective
pre-ejaculatory state.
peduncle fluke
held oddly still.
left eye closed.
eye opened.
peduncle fluke
moved gently down.
inevitability.
positive stimuli
overcome inhibitors,
exciting neurons
in the spinal cord,
relaying signals
to the brain,
prompting secretion;
motor efferent discharge.
womp. womp.
contraction of
the epididymis
and vesicles;
involuntary pumping
of the bulbocavernosus.
dense seminal fluid
ejected from the tip.
pulsive emission.
muscle stretched up.
(all this repeated twice.)

Man said things not

After the splash in *Hustler*, that was that.
Forget it. We were more than sex. This place,
which liquid hasn't lapped in forty years,
was more: we raised three daughters here.
But sometimes, still, sat in my patterned TV chair,
no polythene in sight, I catch reflections.

Altered States? I didn't get a line in *Altered States*.
That was all John in tanks, half-nude,
a raging monk's magnetic selfishness.
He throbs into his caveman form like lumpy bread,
then flirts with phasing into sentient light.
Love pulls him back, at last.

Mike Nichols thought that love explained it, too.
He married us; gave Peter his own partner;
let us learn and live, despite the fact
we taught a living creature its first lie.
The ball is bad — redeemed beneath Ben Franklin's bust.
More palm-frond beach huts, though, and more verandas.

Worst of them all is this, uploaded to
your stupid website: *Maui, Earth.*
Your disco suit, your coonskin cap — a broken brain,
happy by then to simply find an audience.
A wunderkind who soured into a charlatan,
swimmer who never heard the calls from shore.

Extraction, not love, is the shape I recognise.
You mining anything in the universe —
space, Polynesia, karma, chemistry —
if it could keep you talking. He can't speak.
I don't know where his body is.
You only know the ones you think you've hurt.

Come and See the Songs of Strange Days

31/03/2021

SJ Fowler

L'enfant Sauvage

I was that ratboy from the forest
which was a big black mound of hair.
I haven't got a clue why.
I was the locked gate that will greet all children
the French basket, the noisy sock puppet.
The spectacular poems portraying spectacular beasts
in a paradise called revenge.
Who washes? Who would want to kiss mine jaw?
The overrated natural state of me,
is a little dog I loved that drowns in the sink.
This demonchest of the forest makes sense in savagery.
I want to bite everything and eat some of it.
I want your leg.
I want a nice tucked in curling ball and roll.
I want a cruel black dog tempting return.
I want to read, and then build about.
I want nice shops and promenades
and the fake smells of armpits.
I want the very process of perfumes from all over.
I want the liquid other bodies produce all over me in private.
I want to bring what I know from the darkness of the trees
into your lives.
Having learned more from the stupid, says Montaigne,
I now know less.

RELEASE: 26 February 1970
DIRECTOR: François Truffaut

Little Otik

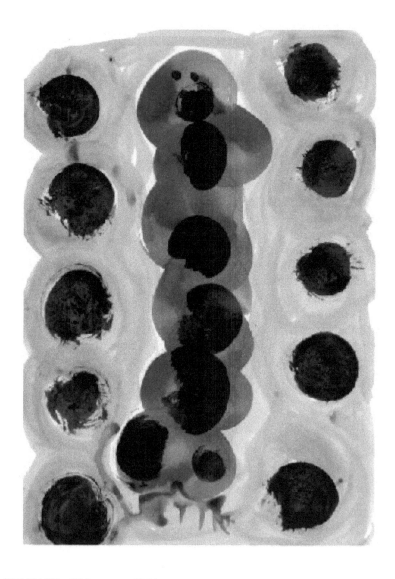

RELEASE : 25 January 2001
DIRECTOR: Jan Švankmajer

Pierrepoint

The job of the most closely guarded secrets,
there is no sense to prolonging the agony.

Those who have paid the price are innocent now,
or so says the man who attempts leaves himself beyond the
noose.

Something beneath feet, disappears. A lever, a switch.
A suggestion that one follows me.

Fairness isn't weakness, for if one wishes swiftly,
that should be granted. It's mercy.

The world should know our executions were the most efficient and
humane.
Without shot, or strangling. With the separation of vertebrae.

The time for a brew that must be denied, for who wants to fall
behind?
The leaner the man, the shorter the drop.

RELEASE: 12 September 2005
DIRECTOR: Adrian Shergol

Jurassic Park 3

ALAN

RELEASE: 20 July 2001
DIRECTOR: Joe Johnston

Peter Pan

with Prudence Bussey-Chamberlain

to have a fat and irate father
in a room with the nursemaid
dog pouring tonic into spoons
and licking paws medicinal properties
pan pirate poppycock
it all starts in the stories
we get too old for
where the hook is on
your left hand not right
now George now George
sent to a room of his own
where the nursery & the puppy
stop at nothing but building blocks
and errant skates and children are
kidnapped when the window is left open
so call the police and see how well
they never never land
to be a lost boy is so
poet to brawl and fight
fashion weapons out of supermarket
chain go underground
& mystical appropriation where
the substance nights are long
heavy lit up moments
to be a beat
is so lost and violent shanking
in the jungle where here bottle tops
smashed necks a jugular in leaf-green
dress
mismatch rhythm of clothes
mob mentality and gangs that war
eye-patched and one-handed
you carry your markings forever
which are only a trauma in ink
you can tell us stories
and we will call you Mother

you cannot be lost or beat or boy
women tell their stories with their
ovaries; they must; they need to
n the experimental fairy
nightmares syncopate to dawn
green reverse tulip dresses
Tinkerbelle of trouble
beauty, where in the affective
light of an emotional disco
I was in love with Tigerlily
this whole time
one day, a lantern, ablaze with
reconciliation under the bell
jar turned red glow with anger & trying
in opportunity for flight like jet
or standing in your window
posed, hands on hips, and legs a step apart
the bell-ringing heroes are always
a Judas and pendulous flower-like
move towards their fates, resigned.
with your dangerous metal hand &
your distant look
piratical and a crocodile
on your shoulder; here is the tick of a
time-bombing around the landscape
so old beat so faux
looking all bourgeoisie with that
plumey hat and knee high boots
when the ship is air authority
tight with planks and yoga
downward dog the right hand man
to time's rising sun.
the cabin boy is the one true fairy
in a world of wings
until you believe
until you clap
until you say it aloud
all of us will be dying

RELEASE: 27 July 1953
DIRECTORS: Hamilton Luske, Wilfred Jackson, Clyde Geronimi

Acting Out/chem & other poems

31/03/2021

Peter Scalpello

after us,

                        there was
a boy from romania. fingertips itching i ran
through his densely tousled crown that bore
fragments of a political self-derision. escaping
through the mouth his tongue tapped
upon sorrow, my kisses between drags of a
shared roll-up in the doorway that held us in
a moment of conjecture.

                there was gus. he was nice & uncertain
                of how to exploit it, his form a thick stem
                budding up out from the dancefloor of the gay
                club where we had our first date. funny, he had
                on a football shirt (i don't know what team) as if
                it testified to manhood, or something. in him
                i recognised a rationale for sexual currency
                assigned to 'straight acting'; a make-believe
                acceptance to one's singular expression of gender.
                the irrelevance of it all. we partied
                an eliminated seduction among tourists from happier
                places, got carried away, carried
                out the building.

                        after gus there was
                        a boy from germany. we didn't date.
                        his eyes dulled with virescent intent,
                        which i stared into while giving him
                        head. deep in the pupils, they seemed to say
                        i have a girlfriend.
                        he blocked me on whatsapp after
                        & i didn't hear from him again.

tend
er

oppressed &
hypersexual,
i

question
what's the
link

between
violence &
homoero

ticism as the
boiler churns.

you fucking
love me &
say

it again,
hard knuckle

my back so
sheets
dampen in

taps to the
romance of

sacrifice. the
rumour of

sobriety
allows no
ritual, so

our love is
not default.

my tiny
existence this

headstand &
tongue with

your dna.
carry it like

rainwater
weighs down
the

river, like we
get all dress

ed up &
then can't
leave

the house.
how can you
say

love so much
although i'm

not enough?
how can

don't tell
anyone mean

that was all
i've ever

dreamed of

fruit bowl

a guy at work narrates to me his hamartia) he recounts
that one day last year he'd smoked crystal) & had sex
fourteen times with about eight) different people off an
app) he came down with syphilis & now has to limit
himself) it's five a day for a reason, he said) after he's
finished reflecting, i take) myself to the staff bathroom)
to pee) at the urinal i consider my penis & suddenly i'm)
repulsed by it, like my anatomy specifically) represents a
cumulative suffering) my strange antenna, the sum of all
man's compulsion) i put my dick back & sit chastely at
my desk for the) rest of the afternoon; a body with a
penis, observing) the trials of others with the same)
surely enlightened, i question which is an addiction)

which is an addiction ?

little soy sauce fish bottle
    fixed with GBL,
        pleasure buds an unbound nozzle
            spouts vitreous, a miniscule relief

invisible, really squeeze down
        your eager thumbs &
            was it even there?

           what's 2ml to
                man, tattoos that score the width
                    of a heaving torso

                    one lucid bream to ravage
                        inhibition, subdue
                          dysfunction, arrest
                            your forever fervent
                        aorta,

                        arrest forever your—

                    little zesty puddle of
                impetus, distilled

                we drop we do it with
                irony

call out

you led me descending
stone to a doorway that advised obligation
i indulged cumulative proximity
& chemical nerve to galvanise
a performed assurance of motive
your mattress arthritic upon the
encroaching crimson carpet
expressions of predestination implicated a kindling
adrenaline extraneous to lust but in fact
apprehension
horizontal i reasoned the dichotomy
of coveted pleasure & just wanting to cuddle
that confused craving for intimacy
could we just hug for a minute i said as our noses
touched to behold but a freudian blur

or was it
could you get me a drink?
you tucked your erection to the groin
of your jeans & left for rum &
ice a pipe & a pipette
of G i slumped
across the bedroom wall back bare
& sweaty my peripheral form
clinging to the affected
gloss of a photograph

New Years Eve

31/03/2021

Annie Muir

Vatersay

I grew up here in another life
in a white house full of brothers and sisters

We used to watch planes landing on the beach
Mum had long hair then cut it short

I came here to think about my self
but all I can think about is him

A man on the beach who looks washed up
packing bits of rubbish into a plastic bag

I walk uphill through fields of purple clover
towards a big abandoned house

The same man welcomes me, takes my coat –
drops it to the floor

offers me champagne – an old boot
introduces me to his wife – a pile of bricks

and invites me to dinner – I can only imagine
what's on the menu

I politely decline and walk back outside
pretending to close the door behind me

I've been coming here since I was a child
Me and Katie left food out for the fairies

and woke up to a thank you note in fairy handwriting
I wrote the note and even fooled myself

Palindrome

She ate her breakfast backwards, *crunch*,
spitting toast back on the plate and scraping butter off.
She got into bed and slept, woke up,
and went to the pub. All her friends were there –
shouldn't they be at work? –
she couldn't understand what anyone said
but acted like she could. A man with black hair
sat outside. He talked with his hands so was easier to hear
and he conjured cigarettes from ashtrays.
She went to the library and pretended to read
from back to front like Japanese,
went home and ate her breakfast, *crunch*,
got into bed, slept, woke up, picked up her phone
and it rang – *MUM* – she answered and it sounded like

the end of the world. She tried to ignore
reversing cars and dust and hair clinging
to her body. She closed her eyes and saw
a photo: of her mum, dad, brother, sister, her,
and an inflatable killer whale, in a swimming pool,
treading water. *Children are time made solid,*
her mother said, *atomic clocks...*
Atoms weren't supposed to split up, so it was a shock
when they did. The children were all teenagers by then
and not very solid – her mother hung up
and she tried to hold on to the image. A black hair
from the floor landed on her shoulder and she brushed it
away. She tried to remember what happened the night before,
she only drank two pints of *1864*.

Ruth

We stood on a bridge
and a train went under
our legs. We waved
and the driver
beeped. We endured
rivers and barbed-wire
because Ruth said
ten people a year are killed
by charging cows. We saw
Mam Tor bus stop.

The top was windy. We got a photo.

I chased Ruth down
pretending to be
a cow. We hitched back
with two old men listening
to classical music who said
our little legs must be
exhausted.

Seven Postcards

for Amber

The headrest on the plane said: 'Have a nice time here, you are nearly there.' Here there are buses called FINNAIR and the metro looks like a cave, with chalk-white mooses on the walls. We've seen singing policemen perform, and found a message scribbled on the red bricks of an empty factory: 'I was here in 1967'. I'm feeling seasick. See you soon

Through the hostel window I can see a woman wrapped in a duvet – it's next-door to a strip club. Yesterday we learnt about the Baltic Way and walked down tired roads and followed a girl drawing her dog into the shallow sea. At dusk we watched tower blocks from a rock, my teeth chattered and Elton John sang don't let the sun go down on me. See you soon

Today we saw peeling buildings and I bought a second-hand pink flower print dress. You might not like it. An old woman helped me zip up the back in the toilet queue and smiled as if she knew. We dressed up a naked statue in our clothes. All the patterns here make me want to live somewhere else. See you soon

We are trapped indoors because it's raining. In a little art shop a man asked us if we wanted to see "seven paintings about feelings?" and then he went through them one by one: "this one's pain, you know, when someone hurts you, you feel pain? This one's anger, you know, when someone hurts you..." This card is 'tears', I bought it for seven litas. See you soon

I can't move but soon I will have to catch a train. Last night we went to a bar with damp red fur on the walls and a man told us a story about his two front teeth. He said they were fake because once his mum was on the phone and he was nagging for her to change the channel so she threw the remote to him and it knocked them both out. See you soon

I am in the town where Miffy was born. We bumped into someone from our old secondary school who's starting university here, and we found a wine shop with his name so we sprawled outside it on a bench with a silver cat, and made a comic strip where the cat evolves into a human. There are frogs in our hostel's garden that bleep like digital watches. See you soon

I have been here before. My parents asked me if I wanted to go to Anne Frank's house or a houseboat museum and I chose the houseboat. So I went this time to make up for my wrong decision. She had cut out pictures from newspapers and pasted them onto the walls: Greta Garbo, Elizabeth of York and a chimpanzee tea party. See you soon

Enxaneta

In Barcelona it is 38 degrees
and a little girl screams with mimicked joy –

she is all eyelashes, all eyes,
all teeth and gums and tongue.

I hate her through the eyes of her big sister:
half a plastic broken heart tied around my neck,

I climb a fence to watch the *castellers.*
They huddle, arms up as if reaching for a throat,

others climb them like stairs, feet clinging to backs
like tadpoles on their first legs,

it doesn't stop, more like ants than people
but with muscle and bone and white trousers,

two little girls heading for top,
one takes her place below, the other

is no longer a child but the star
at the top of a Christmas tree,

her arm pointing up is the man on the moon,
a clock striking midnight on New Year's Eve.

She slides down the legs of her supporters,
relieving the mountains of tension from their shoulders.

Valour

30/04/2021

Emma Hammond

Fog

There is a decent amount of stillness
in snow, and also in the yellow of daffodils.
It would be easy to say they remind me of you,
but they don't. The crown of each
burns. All around, people

are effortlessly people, some elsewhere.
Poets are ghosts. It is not especially
romantic. Stillness and the urge to participate,
hoping the snow sits- casting out lines, always
wonky, the agony! Sounds good does it.

Yet right at the crux, bright amber. Suspended,
knowing our faces are lunatic gaps in some
bottomless armour. So far into absurd that
cash is unfathomable, hearts birthing
bright from our sleeves like hernia. Still,

the need to be a part of it, to have existed-
to never forget that we are slipping away
all miracle. Vivid and extra, skin and light,
experiments in weather. To touch, to write it
right. Staying open in the only way we

Blue

Across a reddening ocean
of tangled cables, sinew,
or by a white bloody van upon
a bridge that does not reach,

one by every one the kids
get pulled like toyless crackers.
Old moons, familiar soils. still,
the crones warn us in bullets

love is abstract, childish.
We suffer their unreal flag
in swathes of crime tape-
hyperbole, traditions of sickness,

a terrible romance, these apes.

September

Waking in September is
half great half death-
the sexy low sun that pierces
your eyes and the wailing

Of the washing machine. O
sadness, the softener is all
gone, the trees are killing
themselves all over the place-

You are wedged in your bed
like a loose tooth. The imminent
bare-sole pain of the coldy tiles-
the depression! Smudges on

The wall, your mouth, the alarm-
a bastard. White skies undress
in the tsk tsk of autumn rain,
and the summer cries *evil*! Dead.

Charlotte
poem for a gosh-daughter

Bean-toed
wonder of the Copt
and tiniest
marsh-ling,
bright eyed
supergirl
tied
in bluebells
& sea-lavender-
pink as a
an Essex sky.

for Aldous

In the pink room we have found
each other- you in the blue sling
and I deep in the dreams that
I have for you. It is raining post
heatwave and I am glad your tiny
feet are cold as shells, my heart-
beat pressed up hard against
your ear. Nothing can touch us

now. Your duckling hair is real
as you are, I never thought we'd
get this far. I had you in mind for
so long you're still made up, an
unbuilt world. Sometimes you
chirp and I realise you're here,
hot little hands in a grip, how
serious you are. When your eyes

open they are in flint, intent,
certain in some cold burning that
you've been here before. Wrap me
up in that, I like it. I like you a lot
small policeman. You are the icing
on the ocean- a dot! And when you're
asleep I transcribe every breath,
golden crest, tiny bird, new entire.

Unravelanche

30/04/2021

Jon Stone

The Ghost with Trembling Wings

gol

             den

toad   har

                  le

                          quin

       frog

            flam

                boy

   ant

     ly

             col

                   our

                 ed

    temp

       orary

                             pud

                    dles

Imagine a maker of jewellery, conjuring
a bangle in the shape of an amphibian;
              pouring in the hot, molten metal,
     burnishing and polishing the cooling cast.

Biggles in the Jungle

                Rif
                    le   Pet
                                                rol

        tank   Luc
                                    ky
                                            shot

                Glan
            cing
                                blow   A

            brisk
                        fire
    A
                                    jag
                                        ged
                hole
                        Pink
            dawn

Then, round a shoulder of rock far below them,
appeared that Tiger, the mounting sun.
Algy emptied his revolver
                    into the animal's sleek flank.

Ice Station Zebra

                                 Haz
                                     ards
oil
        huts
                              gale-
                                  for
                                          ce
      lamp
                  lips
    whis
                            ky
        men
                  Doc
                              Skin
           bulk
      he
                          ads
                  jet
grip
                            dam

The ice sloped up sharply to a ghostly
hooped steel skeleton, fire-charred
goggles and snow-masks.
No ridges, no hummocks, no crevasses.

The Observer's Book of Masqueraders

Gather
        ing   satin
                      sti
tch
            godd   ess

    kind   ling
                    mater
    ial
                                dots
        coxcomb
                    school
    ro   om
        smo   ocked
                bed

cape   scal
            loped

                    neck

He unclenched his herringboned hem,
and showed her the crushed letter.
        She dragged one long thread through
his burning mouth.

The Woman in Drēama

```
wornas                              widsceope
        Ah,           de           ar!
   bi        noman        hāten    best
                  ānsta                gra
                        pan                    ce
   dare        say              gemet fæst
      lufsum        with              out
u              tte           ri                  ng
            a
                  word        wlitig
   and      wynsum                   trif
                                  les
         hand
              kerch
                     ief   cynes
                             tōlum
         spy
```

This was the Secret, and it was
her fyrngeflitan. Swēttra and swīþra, that last misty
death-swoon. Scattered over the table.
                  Swā bi∂ scinnena þēaw.

Dreamlands

30/04/2021

Razielle Aigen

Imprint

"Tu ne sais ni où tu vas ni pourquoi tu vas ; entre
partout, réponds à tout . . ."
  — Arthur Rimbaud, Mauvais sang, Une saison en enfer

"You do not know where you are going, nor
why you are going; enter anywhere, reply to anything."
  — Arthur Rimbaud, "Bad Blood," A Season in Hell

Enter anywhere. Be diaphanous.
Make soft your shape.
Cat. Cow. Cobbler. Shell.
Let the softness, the inkiness of you
settle in in the intaglio. Seep
like walnut oil into carved coper
ridges of line and form.
Leave an impression.
Leave an imprint,
a mark of your body.
Be heavy enough.
Be here enough. Decide
on something and then make it
soft, translucent.

Become a feather and float.
Become a winter moon and shimmer.
Become iridescent as amaranth.
Give a blood curdling balk — go ahead, wake them!

Now imagine sunlight glittering on the snow.
Now imagine sunlight dizzily drinking an open field.
Now imagine a wooded creek encircled by a thousand shapes
of death, shades
of the lily-livered that lay dormant within us, now departed
so that we may recoup,
so that we may regain our ruddiness and footholds
in rebirth.

Learning
to bear the radiance of it all.
Every swollen ego and effective trust.
Every malevolent gold-digger and virgin Mary Magdalene.
Every last revolver and open heart.

And I wonder, is it possible?
Can rage be distilled enough to be abandoned?
Just checking,
because it's pisces season and the light of the crepuscule is mutable.
These signs are minuscule, but please, read them carefully.
Hold on to the banisters.
Something is shifting.

Antediluvian Forest

You can see the old growth forest as a body
the naked November branches, the dendrites
of your neurones
the heavy of oak trunks, the coarseness
of your enormous thighs.
Their roots, your roots. Your underground
rhizomic unconscious, tangled
in the nodes of a karmic thicket.

You can see the body as a temple, primeval
with a diadem of trees beaming on a hilltop
brushing the clouds crowded in
like upside down mountains
illumined tangerine from within, reflected in a pristine
clearwater lake, its source a rushing waterfall
an outpouring, a rent in the hardness
of your petrified rock face.

Dusk. The hour between dog and wolf
in which doubt corrodes the heart
the brilliance of the day
conceding that it can too be beautiful to become
less beautiful, beautiful to grow old. A shift
towards nightfall. The weirdness
of aging. Running, we lie
that we like how it makes us feel
when really we like how it makes us look.
Vibrant, youthful, eternal.

The forest path is soft and supple, forgiving
every breathless heal-toe stride of vanity, absorbing
the shock and anxious mourning of a bird's nest
chest, burrowed in patterns of ancestral grief
home to a fragile, unhatched
speckled egg and a sunken heart

not relatable to anything actual
a deceptive residual depression of deep time
nourished by not doing anything
to decrease its volume or soften its cardiovascular impact.

And maybe there's meaning
in the weirdness. Or maybe it's just weird.

You wake up and wonder. What if
everyone decides in hive-mind collectivity to love
you all at once, despite your compulsive running
despite the tropes of your mind transfigured
by rock knots of inherited guilt and anger and
your congenital personality defects daisy-chained into an aura
around you that makes them say *boy, she's moody!*

On some level, you know
being natural is just as much a contrivance.
On some level, you know
you'll keep running in the forest.

Sweet pea, zucchini, lemon balm & lupine

asters & thistle, clematis & lily, beets
& arugula, lettuce & thyme, oregano, mint
basil, phlox & carrots, radishes, spinach, raspberry
tomatoes & cucumber.

A garden lined with amoral daffodils
uptight crocuses and strewn

with stinking drunk peonies
too bone weary to remove the mascara streaming

down their cheeks, no shame
in their explosive tattered bursts

of hysterical pink anger
and general over-the-top too muchness

all tangles and untameable, wild
and without care

for the mundane burdens of being.
Laissez-faire bonnes vivantes, couldn't care less

that we had just re-emerged
from yet another Mile End winter, only just barely

scraping by under a muted darkness
cast over the hemisphere

in which we hadn't banked
on the hollowness of bones becoming

another person's structural integrity
transplanted and unearthed

amidst a forgiveness radiant and mellow.

In our permacultured heart
of hearts there is always this sense of almost

belonging, though everything about it
feels more like longing

for a reality that we're slowly, only
now reconfiguring ourselves around.

A rusted train yard covered over in white
silence waits for

spring, thawing its way into beginning.
We'll look back at the snow covered tracks

that separated us all winter long
from Little Italy and think to ourselves

how well we kept our balance
between how much everything mattered

and how easy it was to erase.

Dream Borderlands

I am not your Iphigenia
oh father, you

who are not here anymore
to dispense judgement

disapproval or blessing
willy nilly like the wind when she wildly interferes

taking with her what she whirlingly wills, unhinging
doors right from their frames

carrying off to oblivion anything
not sufficiently tied down —

she shows no mercy.
dear you, father

I am not a sonnet but you can
if you must, interpret these dream borderlands

in which your future self is watching you
in your endless sleep

in which you win your war over the wind.
the ruins now seem fitting as a starting place.

k, bye

if the pale morning
moon were still
to faintly linger
with sky-blue sluicing
through her irregular
rice paper surface
as a lasting impression
made in a subjunctive mood
by the night;
then the sky (as a context
for the conditional)
will become paralyzing
contingent on doubt
and the quietude
of a palaeolithic night.

(the time long before
we came to know ourselves)

here
in this pale place
of if
of other
of opacity
admittedly
none of your lobster-coloured geraniums
go unnoticed.
flower by passing flower
you leave no broken hearts.

k, bye you say
and I wonder
how many lifetimes
we'll dream through this
fading facade
of night.

Rude Mechanical

31/05/2021

Jack Warren

Prospero Returns to the Island

He grows kale, red onions
and listens to the goldfinches flitting
from the telephone wires. When night comes
he takes solace in the laying of firewood
in cross-sections against the corner of the hovel
so there will always be warmth whenever he demands it.
When he grows sick of the sound of his own breathing
he takes long walks to the new ferry terminal
or back along the irrigation ditches to the pub.
Here he nurses pints of Guinness, curses the tourists
their photos on the cliff. Often he remembers
his daughter and the grand-kids he's not allowed to visit
then later, stumbling home along the tow-path, he pauses
to see the red light of a Boeing passing overhead.
The world becoming smaller, and ever more distant.

Aubade After Illegal Rave

All the day's allotted joy was spent
last night, dancing in a limestone
echo chamber on the Mendips,
and I don't know whose idea it was
to jerry-rig speakers in a disused quarry,
nor why sleepless and mouth-sore we're trying
to walk the Roman road back to my flat
but there's dog violet trembling in the dawn heat
we can hear city cars thundering along an A-road
we're too diluted to even sweat effectively
and all the birdsong feels percussive.
Let us hold this day at arm's length then,
draw the curtains against the fabulous sun
and huddle together under an ancient duvet,
because though the coming hours will not be kind to us
yesterday we were liquid in the burning moonlight
and all else is superfluous.

Telemetry

Though the science of telemetry
is in it's infancy, already
there are transmitters so tiny
as to be worn like rucksacks
on the thorax of foraging bees.
Each one, though capable of sending
data of flight path or flower choice
is nothing next to the unalterable
darkness by which larger satellites,
hurtling through our universe,
return images of chemical and colour.
So if sometimes it feels like we are moving
further apart, think of us instead
as twin components of signal and receiver
each reliant on the distance overhead
both navigating by the silences in between.

I hope its not too loud for you

After eight months of long distance
I am a stroppy minor demigod
from a lesser Greek myth, shouting
your name across the ocean between us.

My voice cracks the hull of a Navy Destroyer
stationed in the mid-Atlantic, then breaks
against the Eastern Seaboard like a hurricane.
'Good' I think, 'Good' as I shout it again
and the Pentagon goes to defcon 5.

I shout 'I miss you!' 'Come back'
and the sound wave forces a twenty-two
yard touchdown pass backwards
into the Patriots own end-zone.

In Portland Maine thirty-thousand lobsters
fly through the air like a biblical plague
and in south Florida my voice shoots an alligator
from the swamp like a leathery torpedo,
obliterating the drive-thru of a Burger King.

In the ensuing chaos headphones and earplugs
become the most looted items while skirmishes
between tinnitus sufferers frequently turn violent.
Two weeks later the president appears on television

declaring war on sound itself, making reference
to it as 'the ideological enemy of this great nation'.
People begin to whisper to each other.
The country's most prominent opera singers,
firework makers and drag racers are all rounded up

and quietly frowned at. I grab a bullhorn and a raft
and start paddling, but in this new dictatorship
of silence where the pledge of allegiance is signed
and the national anthem has been replaced

by milder forms of reflection, how will you know me?
How will you ever find me if not in the noise
and chaos I can cast across the sea?

St Petersburg at New Year

For Anya

As we walk along the frozen Neva
listening to the snow's gathering silence
I think of all the exhausted Januaries
I've had to greet alone in one room flats,
or staggering home through the oily rain,
strung out from fifteen hour shifts, the year
only a sluggish promise of much the same.

But the Baltic wind is dying off around us
fireworks are exploding over the Hermitage
and I would like to hold their lighted tails
between finger and thumb, then blow,
so that instead of each bright cluster of colour
booming, flaring and falling, they would
glide across the sky like dandelion seeds
caught in the momentum of some irresistible
force of air and joy, moving as one towards the new year

Springing from the Pews

31/05/2021

Day Mattar

springing
from the pews

he was seventeen

i was six

*it happened
in my bedroom*

                      but

*it didn't hurt
      i wasn't
forced*

i should hate him!

cross the road   to a church

the organ   sings

the stained glass   hums

rain
        riots
on the concrete
my fists
            bounce
off the arched
wooden door

storming the walls
the hems of my corduroys
soppy   slapping
my ankle

I want the priest to read verse
while I sob

my little lamb pushing itself out
    to candlelight
    its white body   springing
    from the pews

[ACT I]

[*spotlight   LAMB, centre-stage   shearing its own wool*]

VOICE TWO: [*left*] it was a
VOICE THREE: [*right*] a fantasy!
VOICE FOUR: [*behind*] he made-
VOICE FIVE: [*above*] he made it up!

LAMB: look
[*barks*] look!

this skin [*shorn wool, wilting*]
this skin [*blood shot eyes*]

[*table drops from the sky   chair drops from the sky   human body drops from the sky with pen*]

and you! [*rears*]
for nineteen years
carrying his cock like a torch.

VOICE ONE: was it rape?
VOICE SIX: it was rape!

[*above   a murmuration of origami birds   oscillates*]

[JOURNAL]

sex clicks
into place along my spine, bends me over the sink.
brushing my teeth after a fuck, worried about the blood on the brush.
the tui and the bellbird's chorus, alien, through the window.
there's an alternate dimension where this didn't happen,
one where i stayed in New York, living above the little cupcake bakery,
a boy with turquoise hair
brings me turquoise roses.

maybe sex isn't dark there.
do i use a condom? am i as lucky? did i stop cutting? maybe
it's worse. twisted by ghb and crystal, limp
in a gimp sling, cold
sweat dripping from the ceiling. coming to
in a dark room. somewhere, i'm on PrEP.
can i afford it?

[ACT II]

[spotlight   centre stage, LAMB on interrogation stool]

CCTV CAMERA: [groans into position] your mum
is just on the other side of that door [purrs] there is nothing
to be afraid of

[...]

would you like some apple juice?

[distant rumbling]

can you tell us what happened?

[dry earth splits]

did he promise to give you something?

[a field of sunflowers ignites into screams]

did he say something bad might happen?

[a swan cracks the whip of her neck]

do you have anything else you'd like to tell us?

[the stage fractures and drifts]

[LAMB drops a pebble into the audience   the audience ripples   the ripples grow
and grow]

springing

from the pews

following cock
into the beach toilets
at pt. chevalier   jasmine
steaming on the fences

cold knees
on damp green tiles   jaw
locked in prayer
at the gloryhole

                    but
it wasn't cock i followed into my bedroom
          it was love
               but it wasn't love
          it was rape
     was it rape?

outside   two blackbirds hop
across blossom scattered pavement
another knocks back a worm
tilts its head

Nothing of the Month Club

30/06/2021

Jeff Alessandrelli

"The problem of America is my body."

after Alice Notley

Every gustatory pleasure
is a field
that will one day fail
to provide pasture.
Or
I'm worried
about my belly fat again,
home alone every night,
dusting,
doing dishes,
my 34th winter.
Noisier the leaves
seem to get
the deeper into November
one goes,
muddier the sun.
Suddenly under-
dreaming
my days away,
all worthwhile interests
waning,
my favorite book
merely
the girl with the best ass
in the neighborhood,
the only poem
that tempts me
her boyfriend
working out in his apartment
in the gloaming's half-light,
his phosphorescent 6 pack abs.
Insomnia's eternity,
glutton for drudgery,
hours later I'm up
before dawn,
thinking about the sign

outside my favorite taqueria
that reads
No Shirt, No Shoes, No Problem;
the way the shards of afternoon
sun seem
to make it glow
neon-bright.
There I sit at my corner table for hours,
ignoring the herds of cars and buses
that pass by and pass on.
Outside this fiefdom
the problem of America
is my body
but inside I am swallowing
so many different poisons
at such breakneck speed
as to actualize myself
invincible.
So it matters little
how important my mouth is
to my throat, my lips
to my gums, the charbroil-seared
sound of my voice
to my belly's girth.
Walking home at dark,
noisier the leaves seem to get
with each step.
And pockmarked and pristine,
looming larger and larger,
the moon.

"I Lost my Virginity to a Rainbow."

Older than me by what seemed to be a beguiling amount of years, my pen pal from England fancied himself a visionary of sorts, sending letters that began "Last week I lost my virginity to a rainbow skying above Trinity College in Dublin, the heavens desiccating their eternal glories for treasures that only lie beneath." Lasting just two exchanges, our correspondence ended when my mother read the above and, her eyes housing small fires, two dull blue flames, angrily called my father at work.

The Third Sitting Room

For years I dreamed of writing a novel about napkins. Although the book would encompass other themes and topics, from competitive archery to one hapless dreamer's quest for an ancient stash of Austrian gold galleons, the central concern of the text would be napkins, with each character contemplating just what a napkin means to both them and the world at large. For Galván, ample in his minorness, a napkin is simply a thoughtless means of tidying up his face and person after a meal of any size. More original and idiosyncratic in scope, for Yana a napkin is something to study rather than use. The napkins provided by the host or restaurant, of course, tell far more about the nature of the attendant design (aesthetics; utility) than the actual food might ever hope to. She parses this assertion endlessly, chapter by chapter, from linen squares to cheap paper cocktails. It's the hierarchical that Felicity, the novel's central character, is most interested in. Working in Acquisitions in the Slavic Studies Department at an Ivy League university, she regularly travels to Eastern Europe. There she makes note of what she doesn't see—namely, napkins. Although the places she visits are often far cleaner than anywhere in North America and, even in the midst of the intermittent societal upheaval and cultural transformation, the citizens of those places are more spotless and kempt than any others she has witnessed the whole world over, Felicity rarely if ever spies a cloth or paper napkin (recycled or otherwise) to accompany all this order. Meals are deliberate, rushed or ornately involved—and cleanly consumed no matter which. Becoming obsessed, Felicity searches and searches, her lack of progress somehow confirming her hypothesis that napkins are to slovenliness as oxygen is to air; expectation begets actuality.

One day Felicity wakes up and studies the heretofore ignored crumbs on the edge of her lonely hotel writing desk and, aged just 44, collapses dead from exhaustion, vintage terra cotta napkin ring in one hand, pristine four ply dinner napkin in the other. It is at this point that the novel would, stridently and impercepti- bly, begin to cohere into a künstlerroman of a kind, albeit one that refuses the satisfaction of an earned maturity. The years pass unevenly in dreams, ¼ flying, ¼ drowning. After eating my schnitzel I wipe my face on my lapel, first the right, then the left. Ceaselessly I reload the pencil in my head, clear off the tablet in my mind. Intoxicated by a future. ¼ landlocked, ¼ tongue-tied. ¼ besought by the research of wonder. I could see it all so clearly, the way she would walk into a room fingers first, searching; her innocuous jacket, shoes, socks. Once.

Nothing of the Month Club

Most German fairy tales end with the sentence "Not long afterwards, there was an outbreak of the plague," and so the sudden death of a thousand fictional schoolchildren living in the Maxvorstadt proves imagination is a fact, fact with a spurious relationship to the truth. Hey Mr. Police Officer, if you're so smart how come you're only doing your job? Hey Mr. President, if you're so smart how come you're only doing your job? Hey Mr. Prime Minister, if you're so smart how come—. Did you know that in Mexico you have to *pay* to go to high school? Dumb American kids like myself are f-u-c-k-i-n-g lazy. Yesterday I studied the sky for hours, coming away with the realization that I can do nothing I am not against the emotional smear campaign otherwise known as life. I'm too smart. Horizon, cloud, the sky was crowded yesterday. I will mention the dead birds. I will mention the heavy wind. Will mention that what the wind makes out of the air is a bird's burden, wings ceaselessly swimming sky. "Oh a stately pleasure-dome decree/ Where Alph, the sacred river, ran/ Through caverns measureless to man/Down to a sunless sea." Flying is for the birds. Where eagles dare. I ain't no god-damned son of a bitch. Death exists at the border of fact and imagination and some fatal acceptance seals it. Hey Mr. Policeman, if you're so smart—. And so ends the tale of little boy Gunther and Stalvirt, the magical horse that saved all of Munich. Not long afterwards, there was an outbreak of the plague.

Stray

after Ray Johnson

Then I saw a blind woman
in the supermarket
checkout line
with about forty items
in a ten-items-or-less line.
She was maybe 65 years old.
There were a lot of people
lined up
behind her.
6 by my count.
This was at 6:20 PM
on a Wednesday in July,
arguably peak supermarket
shopping time.
I believe that lofty pronouncements
and declarations
are things to disparage
in life, in art
and literature. Mostly.
Like the stray dog
that my neighbor Jim feeds
when he wants to
and doesn't
when he doesn't.
Jim's divorced, in the insurance business,
and I think he owns his apartment
outright. But I have no
real sense of these things
beyond the unwarranted
airs of superiority
that manifest themselves
in cologne onslaughts, bulbous
wrists filled
with too much calcium.
I don't know
dogs, though, not really,
at least not

in the way
that, say,
I know
what it's like to miss
the last 19 bus
on the S Line
and have to hoof it
home on foot,
the darkness a kind of performance
art piece, ascending
while descending.
It doesn't have a name,
the stray. Or maybe
it does, intuits what
to respond to
depending on the offer and situation.
Jim calls it
Here Little Guy,
Here You Go,
There You Go,
All Of It,
Whoa,
Don't Go
Too Fast Now,
There You Go,
That's Alright, There
You Go.
Now. That
Was. There
You Go.
Or doesn't.
That July was so hot,
especially that night.
I could hardly work
on my square breathing, deep
breaths, peaceful thoughts.
The blind woman
took her items out
one by one,
slowly and carefully,
and no one helped
and no one said

anything.
Some shift manager
didn't materialize
to assuage everyone's feelings
and let us leave
or forget.
Stuck, we
just watched.
Bright
fluorescent lights.

Play Lists

30/06/2021

Jessica Mookherjee

Talking

Your mind flows over each neuron and bursts
into a star flower as I watch, all lost for words,
talk unprepared, thick and after hours
you ask me who I am—I wish you were less

familiar, your question helps me lose feral notes
of what comes next; words that stick,
that glow with what comes from being sea sick,
changes in one drift of instant. I wish

I'd not had that last drink, where the wine glass
grows bright, I say oh no oh no it's out of my hands
spilt over sawdust of a south London pub floor
and my dress. We talk and talk about Lacan

Long Walk Home

These are bleak times he wrapped a heavy coat around himself,
said there was a band playing in Gorseinon – did I want to come,
I had no way of getting there without some assistance and would it be safe?
There is nothing safe, there are nuclear missiles about to go off,
don't you know what capitalism is? Don't you know where Mordor is?
I told him I did know – and could I have a lift? He said he wanted to
put make up on and could I help. I was ruby lips and pixie boots.
He was cut off denim jacket and a face of silver and green.
Your mascara is running, I told him. He sighed, It's meant to look
like this, get in the car or we'll be late. I was sandwiched
inside a bohemian rhapsody of boys. These were indeed bleak times

Nevermore

He saw dark flagged ships in me, before anyone else,
Let me catch them for you and they can be our friends.
There were always boys like that, the ones who didn't
play football. Some hints of the devil in him too.
We didn't speak much. I had a raven on my shoulder,
he walked a wolf down the promenade and told
me about serial killers and Charles Manson.
Between us, we knew nothing about heroin
or alcoholics or amphetamines but he had a book
by William Boroughs called Junky, told me to read it.
I read twelve pages and abandoned it, he devoured.
I wasn't allowed to talk to him in school but could meet
up by the woods where he'd give me a tape of all the songs
I should listen to, ones that had the sound of machines,
static, feedback. I turned up with a copy of Melody Maker
and Smash Hits to discuss what they'd written about Lou Reed.
He turned up with half a bottle of Jim Beam, sat on a tree stump,
smoking and read out the lyrics to Berlin as if they were poems,
told me his mother had left and started to cry. I saw gunboats
harboured in his chest, I felt echoes of a man I hadn't met.
He asked me first, before anyone else, and the raven
whispered Go home, this isn't your adventure yet.

Broke

You said you loved me, Impossible Boy, we'd only just met,
you said you wanted to be my dog and I let you lap,

Animal boy, I never let on that night I was secretly Iggy Pop.
You said I was hot and cold girl, blowing bites like September,

I was pout and preen, weaned in a glamour with a swagger,
blissed in the club. I span you, Top-boy, tales of the end

of the world, told you I'd make magic in a champagne glass
and line of coke. I wanted to forget where I was heading,

coral lips, brittle and deadly. Of course I didn't love you,
how easy to un-cure the heart of heat, be covered in tiger musk.

How easy to leave stink at the tube station, not take calls
or objections. Hard light in nightclubs had me in focus,

you were token, a heart break broken, how easy to lie awake
and leave you wanting more. That's it Happening boy,

my scar your wound and I learned what it is to be fuel.
I was sound of car alarm one night. How easy to be cruel.

Cherry-Bomb

That old Mae West thing was brought out when needed.
Tattered feather bower, fur coats and what have you.
Curry flavoured little madam, Phoolan Devi, cholan,

and he, not quite James Dean, liked the spices, the colours,
she tasted jellied eels, cockney good-boy shtick,
and special offers. *Shall we play ration books and gravy?*

He did have a lot of books on war, and an active duty
interest in the snipers on the Russian front. *Little boys
want to be soldiers*, was reprimanded with lectures,
the doodlebugs and upkeeps, for his *cherry-bomb*.

G.I. Joe some nights, collar turned up, smoking Lucky
Strikes and found her singing alone in an old vaudeville bar.
He didn't look in the clean up kit, with the Doughboys
tucked in his mess, that bitter morning after.

and we were so far from the sea of
course the hermit crabs were dead

30/06/2021

Lotte Mitchell Reford

The First Time They Want You.

You are at a funeral the first time a man tells you you've grown into
a fine young woman. Or does he say *Budding*? The man is old.
He is probably related to you but who knows, all old men look the same.
At dinner in the hotel, the meat looks like tongues and tastes like grass,
tastes like braces in someone else's mouth. It has been said recently, *Budding*,
and you can't stop thinking of the word of what might grow from it and from
you, of how last time the family was together like this,
you sat under the table with your cousins and ate and ate
and now you want to go outside and taste the night air,
you want to drink what your mother is drinking, the wine staining her teeth.
You touch the lamb on your plate – press a finger in
to watch the blood snake into your nail. You are laying on hands,
you will think the animal back to life, imagine it coming together at the table,
a surprised sheep wet from rebirth, wool matted. In the hotel room
You hang out of window smoking and your shoulders are cold
above your dress. You are so full of spit and blood and it is moving so fast
and you wonder about if this thing had been open casket,
if you had placed a hand over your grandmother's face and let it all rush
to your palms. You felt the men follow you like they follow food
their eyes yellow and hungry. They want to open dark mouths and take you in
want to stop your photosynthesis, but you have turned your face to the sky
to all the stars visible out here in the country. You blow smoke through chapped lips.
You know there are more stars than you can count; you know the longer you look
the more you will see. You wonder why you decided to look up.
You wonder why you would ever look away.

Safe Sex

I have a system where I ask them, *Are you a murderer?* and it's pretty solid
it's worked every time so far. Normally the boy will laugh and say,
Yes, I have an axe upstairs, or else he will roll his eyes, or I will think he is rolling his eye
at me in the dark. I will want to put a hand over his face, lay my fingertips
over his eyelids and press the heel of my palm into his mouth. Instead usually I wait
and keep my fingers by my side. I let his hand move to mine like he's making
the decisions. Sometimes, though, when I ask, *Are you a murderer?* A boy
will look shocked. He will look so shocked I know he has never thought
about hurting anyone, about teeth digging into his skin and spit on his wrist.
He has never even thought of hurting himself, not even in passing,
not even a little bit, not even a pinch that ends in a twist not even a thumb
curled into an out-flooding bruise or a butter knife pressed into flesh until it turns
white as lard until it turns pink as *What the fuck am I doing* until blood
is drawn despite it being a butter knife. This boy, he has never even drunk
so much he bled all over his white shoes or he did it once and never again
or he at least threw the shoes away, didn't keep them like a trophy like a talisman,
like a lucky rabbit's foot. He didn't wear them at Halloween the next year
like, *Fuck you*, didn't vomit on them this time didn't sink them in mud
and late October mulch. And when a boy looks like that looks surprised
and then says, *No, God no, why would you ask that?* And maybe pulls
me to him in a one armed hug maybe puts his face in my hair,
I don't so much want to come upstairs with him and I have to find a way
to forget the surprise, to forget the story he told me earlier about fishing
with his father and the one about how they named three dogs the same
because his little brother didn't yet understand death and his mum wanted
it to stay that way so I ask him what his dog was called and he tells me
and it's something unimaginative and a while later, in the middle of things,
the things we were headed upstairs to do, I can't help myself I yell, *Call me Fido*,
and I make sure he feels my wet mouth all over him.

Jonas Mekas at the Tate Modern

Someone has fallen asleep in the dark of the gallery;
their snoring reminds me that we all die horribly
and of the time you told me to look out the window at the moon,
the way I said, *the moon is boring.*

On screen the little iron fences in the parks are the same.
Wooly hats are the same.
The baby, like all babies, is covered in spit.
Snow is a nuisance, a joy, the same.
House plants are brown at the edges,
moving, a hassle,
pizza is just the same,
cars are maybe brighter,
striped T-shirts are striped T-shirts,
and the moon hangs in the sky.

It reminds me that we all die horribly and
of the time my father cried because he found a cat
mummified beneath the floorboards of the family room,
how you said *life is boring*
like you were spitting out three olive pits.

Coca cola signs are the same on shop-fronts
and trees are naked just the same.
There is more coal everywhere,

and if life is boring then what's the point?
Unless it's the way the camera drops suddenly
to catch something new
and the world becomes a quilt of colour.

How we all die horribly, and the night that I left you
I got that coffee from a petrol station on the M1,
when I was about to fall asleep at the wheel,
how perfectly a bite comes out of a Styrofoam cup,
a half-moon,

and there's the dirty feet of the the artist's daughter,
the Velvet Underground's first show,
in an apartment uptown, in front of a striped T-shirt that's
a striped T-shirt,
and the way bad dancing is the same, and
light falling in long squares down a hallway is also just the same.

There is Jonas Mekas at 90 still keeping these video diaries,
and there's the itch to leave the restaurant
to write a stupid poem.
There's the decision to stay and talk awhile
over stained napkins

and there's the times I've seen my father cry:
when he was sick, when his best friend jumped from a balcony,
sometimes when I leave.

There's the fact that he found the lost cat at last
and cradled it carefully and laid it on the rug
and called me and told me the story;
how some old heartbreak he had almost forgotten
had been waiting under our feet all along,
out of sight and still the same.

Cat

There was this cat, with one ear missing and a hole
right to its brain. I had never seen a brain like that
before, in a head cracked open. I've seen them in jars
and at meat markets, covered in flies sometimes and blood
everywhere across tiles designed to show it
off, but I'd never seen a brain still in use.
We said nothing as we walked past. The cat
meowed. The cat went about its business and we
went about ours. We were on holiday. The cat cleaned its one ear.
There was a breeze block nearby. We didn't have to say, *should we.*
We knew we wouldn't. It was minutes later, on another street
you said, *maybe we should have put it out its misery.* I said
It wasn't in misery. You said, *It will be, though.*
We went to find dinner, and then the sea.

South for Winter

When I imagine myself rotting it isn't mourning it's a mantra. A lesson in living and letting go. I wonder where roots will grow and what bones they will grasp and snap. Driving through the south the roads are so wide and quiet they draw my attention. After looking for so long at a lack, the overpasses tangled in the sky are striking. Outside Vicksburg, Miss, I see a chunk of one naked and on its side. Its huge steel beams jutt like the ribs of a beast in an oversized elephant graveyard. Everything this far south makes me think of mourning. Not just the swamps and the air like breathing into a palm and the slow way people talk and the bugs; even the welcome centre where we park to sleep seems to be a temporary thing. The attempt at Old South opulence inside is wailing and wailing: there's gilded horses bearing their teeth and too much carpeting in the squat building. I blink and see the place moth eaten. The mounted heads of beasts eaten up, the horses on their sides. Coyotes are curled on the sofas, avoiding the springs that have broken through. They stalk the sidewalk where the guard told me *no dogs, dogs on the grass only*. The motor vehicles that are left are rusted and home to snakes. This is a place that wants to return to before us. This is a place that wants to be let go, a place that imagines itself rotting and it isn't a mantra, it's a plea.

We Are Always & Forever Ending

31/07/2021

Adrian B. Earle

[Mother]

Those of us who could, we felt remorse.
                    Some of us begged, others still, a stalwart.
Few cried innocence until the last,
                    the final inch of rope gave some relief.
Some of us are truly unrepentant.
                    We will kill again, we vowed we would.
Some of us hunger still to have the chance.
                    Given this sudden wakening in the void.
Some of us lift arms we do not have.
                    While one of us despairs unnatural loud,
as loudly as tumescent flesh can howl.
                    One of us, a heart that keens and sobs
cries through a foreign throat of many throats.
                    Stitched to layer vocal folds as petals,
each exhale sounds as gale winds through a roof.
                    Some of us mistake this polyphony,
as further company, in this crude womb.
                    We always thought of hell as dark and cold,
thought sinners from the furthest light of god
                    but those of us of sin are warmed & light.
Salvation? this strange immobile parody of life?
                    Some of us claim we crave the dark.
We yearn to quietly fall back to that dark.
                    We rage that we were promised death, not *this*
this mocking of wholeness, this agony
                    this.

[Moon]

Bright pit
      in dark
            so open.
                  Bright,
                        big hole,
                              warm & bright.
                                  Far as hope

in cold slick
      dark, so high.
            No sound
                  but thump
                      & suck
                            & thump.
                                Far bright pit,

no sound
      just open.
            Dark hope,
                  cold dark
                      hope just
                            Dark. No
                                sound
                                    & this

bright hole,
      so open
            thump & suck
                  & thump & pull
                      & pull & i,
                            i need
                                to reach
                                    that safe

bright hole.
       i need
           to crawl
                back in.
                    i do not
                         want dark
                           & thump

& suck
     & wet.
         & i am wet
           & high
               bright pit
                  is dry
                        i

am small
     & high
         bright pit
           is big
              Dark is fear
                & whispers
                    sound
                       like *night*

Pit is bright,
     whispers
         speak of
            moon

Moon is bright
     & high
         & safe
           & far.
              Night
                is dark
                  & fear
                    & so, i run.

The Couple

Sat across from us, the Couple have been a shining fixture in our dining experience for weeks. Though not quite across from us today, instead three tables away from us & two across. Everyone has noticed.

The couple draw the eye in ways only beings built for each other can. A meeting of split teak whorl for whorl & tanned. Good God they're tanned, the Couple, bronze & happy with a joy that ripples into the others around them as bitterness.

Women pull tight arm folds beneath pits; men suck in paunches pale as mold furred moons & the couple, smiling in their joy, teeth eye ache bright as northern European skies & so tall, She at least 6 foot & Him eye height with the waiter while sat & they're eating

the same all-inclusive buffet delicacies as everyone about them. Yet, in combinations that seem to be the only combinations that make any sense. Everything they eat, the couple, is something I want. They make me...

The Couple makes me salivate for Quinoa, this couple are eating Quinoa & though I have no fond memories, exactly of the taste of Quinoa, yet, as the couple eat it, I need it, we need it, we watch the couple with their ochre bodies eating Quinoa.

& we, the diners, heap the Quinoa onto ice cream, stir it into pints of warm larger, dust the sauce of Duck Chow Mein with the Quinoa & it is delicious. the Couple, the beautiful Couple, both so tall, 9-foot-tall, eyes the hues of split jade & the last oak in oxford, are laughing.

& their laughter is music & the diners cannot help but move to the music. They hate the couple with a love that exhibits itself first as disregard, strained neck muscle & furtive glances, lusty glimpses at a flash of Breast & rippling Back & Lips & Jaw.

Each diner would subsume themselves into that Back, those Breasts, if they could & many do, rising quietly, folding napkins tucking phones into pockets of Bermuda shorts & pressing themselves into the taught calves, the ebony flesh of the couple, so tall, so tanned, & they are consumed.

& the couple, two stories tall now obsidian & shining, they rise & as they rise, they sweep the dining room towards them with the gravity of a dying star & Quinoa streams in sandstorms off plates into their orbit & they tip the waiter with gold & they embrace.

& in their embrace is the world & the beauty of their embrace is like the oceans of the world & diners, some of them overcome by the embrace, begin to weep & strip off bootleg Arsenal jerseys, floral print sarongs. Baring their nakedness to the ocean of their joy, others overwhelmed, simply cease.

Exiting this place with a wistful sigh, leaving their fruit juice & skirt steak to the flies & the couple, their towering magnificence rendering the building to ruin, stride through the wreckage of the dining hall. & the diners, from the rubble, watch them stride.

Across the compound, palms blooming in the cool shadow of their passing, they step over the beach entire hand in hand into the ocean, dark & twinkling eyes blue shifted into the troposphere. Perfect fucking hair, in infinitely tessellating curls. The Couple hand in hand stride into the sea their footsteps quiver the cliffs & turn the sand to glass &
they are beautiful &
they are radiant &
they are gone.

Countrycide

We are not dying.   No.

The cox rot   on heavy boughs fecund rumps
of melon squash   black with flies
& tubers treasured   since the blight   of black four
seven   seed & split   take their chance
in the loam   to be mothers too young.

Badger trundles   from her burrow
butts her hoary head   to the twin barrels
of the cull.   This year
there are no longer cows, the cows   are gone.
Where   more than three elm   stand to-
gether   two are aflame.   The high street
 littered with   acorns mouldering.

A white   van in a lake   settles in the sludge.   We
ignore the frantic   scratch beyond the doors.
We have manners   this   is England.

These days,   the waves   are ruled
by a mothballed carrier   in the Tyne
these days,   Britannia hurls   her spear
into the open   dark

These days,   our coffins   are *English* oak.
These days,   we speak   *English*   in the kebab
shop   *English*   You mug.   Speak it.
These days   are not your days   anymore.
What are you staring at? Got a problem?   Don't look
at me.   Don't *fucking*   look at me.

Oblivion Hymn #4

No birth, nor coming death.
Just cosmic states that build
& pass like weather through
deep time. Imagine, three billion years
of summer rain. I'm trying to say
after all this, that something
else will come. Then after that perhaps
comes something more. The point
(if any must be made)
is nothing really ends
but nothing stays the same.

Collected Pamphlets

31/07/2021

Aaron Kent

Budapest, 2000

--I break your heart.

Dear Artúr,

It was good to hear from you, I also sing in my sleep and wait for cuckoos to march. I am sorry I cannot come home just yet, I was hoping to be with you for your birthday but I will have to miss it this year. How does the sky look in Redruth? Is it still screaming? I have begun drowning myself a little bit every night so that when the flood comes I will be immune.

I searched for the two-forint but only found half. I'd like you to imagine what the Danube looks like so many years after the fact – it is less than it was, it is less than it was. I have written to you twice and you can show your father one. He is not worth a nickname.

Please, send my love to the mines.

Your best friend,

Bampy

Bone Idol

I've never set foot in a pub without boxing gloves and a can of socialism – they wanna split us by those who down pints and those that quaff – the working class is a rainbow is a taught violence – I've never set foot in a pub without a reason to vote – a terraced house tory is still a tory – a terraced house terrorist is a consequence of an iron fist – it takes a parliament to kill a dream and the daily mail to kill a kid – I've never crossed a picket line I didn't love – environmentalism is for the rich I sustain myself on pesticides – we've got slide tackles in our veins and yellow carded kids – thatcher killed my granddad we dream of feeding her asbestos – we've got community and a fried breakfast – put the kettle on – round 2 and no longer sparring – I've never loved a tory and I don't plan on going home

Small, Wingless

I was born on a two piece
pay later, an interest
rate dictated by my
birth centile. I was breeched
in instalments, spread
across the year; my mother

birthed an overdraft limit,
christened the mass in
common tongue. Learnt
to make space a premium,
notched into the damp
like a silverfish pedalling

into the core of us. My
mother's loss in the plaster-
board shaped like every
pet we begged to need
us. My father counting
grief in a shell in the roof,

        the difference between
        me and a mortgage
        is that gutting a house
        takes time.

Lunar Eclipse, Harbour Equinox

During sleep,
our fossil body sleeps during sleep,
I love you side by side.
Lay the fossils down.
I'm sorry. Show mercy,
lie, lie, lie down. Sleep.
Prepare to feed our soul.
Heal, jump us, moor, far.
I hear the heavens are empty.
Be a complete moon, here.
Lie-and-Hold-to-Lie, sleep. Sleep.
Prepare to feed our soul.
Heal, jump, distance, moor.
It bleeds me, the heavens are empty.
Be full of moon, here.

(I'm delaying, I'm delaying)

Lying, holding, sleeping. Sleep.
Prepare to feed the soul.
Healing, depth, distance.
He washed me; the heavens are empty.
Fill the moon, here.

Saint Pablo

Father I'm out of control, I know your
truth is: I'm not visible to you - but
I'm just pretendin' I can see the light.
Confirmation of your footsteps when I'm

crazy on Twitter, is in the night sky.
Your light was influential, family;
brothers down with your mission at home with
my folks – I'm the only one not on your

beams. Please speak to me, say somethin' before
I leave, I wonder where you are, father:
modern day God, scary to see, beaten
to submission and I'm fine now, I guess.

My wife knows my truth, that she visible
to me, her and my kid in the night sky.

THE LIVE ALBUM

31/07/2021

Kat Payne Ware

BACON

To work backwards, I leave
the tongue's wet airstrip.
I travel in reverse with the scalic
whirr of a rewinding
VHS cassette as the fork
takes a taildive back to the plate.
I touchdown in a pool of ketchup
and the opposite of stabbing happens.
The tape speeds up: baked beans
levitate forming a mob in the air
as they are drawn to the lip
of the pan like iron filings
and the toast regurgitates its butter
back onto the hovering knife.
Eventually the tongs arrive
and I am out of the fire
and into the frying pan, buckling
like a red wave before falling
limp and shedding a gradation
of colour. A mammoth
finger and thumb descend
and return me to the packet
where I struggle to find
an antonym for peeling off
from my traymates. Perhaps I cover
them? Perhaps they put me on?

FILLET

I hang from the tongs like a long
pink tongue. A tongue only lolls
when the animal is panting
or dead. Put me down on the tray.
Dream some Frankensteinian science
brings me round with the urgent
throe of defibrillation. I begin to creep
across the counter in the peristaltic
motion of legless things. My direction
of movement makes head and tail of me
— to have direction one cannot just be
meat. I concertina, accordionlike, edge
toward the knife-edge, then rear
into an S like a weasel. My blunt end
is levelled with your face. Neither of us
can speak. Then, in this dream, I find
your mouth, quick kiss, then enter
and worm down your gullet.
I traverse your inner systems. In this
dream, your gullet is a wormhole:
I emerge having pilgrimaged to a new
place. This kitchen is populated
by long pink tongues. On the tray
lies something with legs.

PRINTING

It's all plug and play — print a picture if you want
and up to three lines of text on every primal cut.

Automatically process each carcass by the individual
length. Printing of a health mark is possible.

Performance of homogeneous processing: fixation
belts secure and support us all the way. Easy operation

uniform user-friendly operator panel and trouble-
shooting. Pull us forward by drop fingers, double

sided, synchronised. This is a dynamic concept: even
and clear print result with flexible heads. Cleaning

easy and efficient. High capacity. High
quality carcasses with fixation. Designed

in accordance with the EU and USDA regulations
to meet the strictest demand on health. Fixation

and processing can be performed. All's fair
in plug and play. 750-1,200 carcasses/hour.

BUTCHERING

MEAT RAW MATERIAL

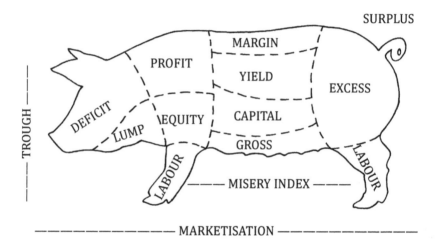

EXSANGUINATION

Torrential would be the word
they'd use on the news, if this
was news. Who'd have thought
the old man to have so much
love in him? He swings me
by the ankles like a happy toddler
who begs for it time and again
whose mother is busy in another
room and not there to say *Put
her down, honey, she'll smack
her   head   on   something
and   then   you'll   be   sorry.
Won't you be sorry?* He fixes
me up with my feet on the rail
in a monkeybar dangle, slides
a blade into my carotid artery
and with this, as if his sticking
were a blessing and I Lazarus
my heart begins to beat again.
This part is crucial. Its beating
disciplines the blood into action.

Plain Air:
An Apology in Transit

31/07/2021

Cat Chong

It is October seventh 2019 and extinction rebellion are rebelling I take a train into London from my home into London I walk to the station that is 9 minutes away from my house nine minutes of movement My body still has a carbon cost of something I take the train into London to see my friends I take the underground between Waterloo and Euston I feel compelled to walk To walk between the University of London institutions for the first time since crossing between 'student' and 'unemployed' UCL Birkbeck SOAS I see my friends and we talk about poetry I take the underground between Tottenham Court Road and Waterloo I take the train back When I arrive at my station Ray my dad has driven to meet me He insists on driving to meet me because it is dark because I am alone because I occupy the shape of a woman because I am disabled and he knows that I am tired insists on driving me home despite the fact that it is close to midnight he drives me home I eat dinner at half 12 I eat the leftovers I left for myself later When I have the energy to cook to eat I am able to be vegan I take a hot drink to bed containing Bimuno powder to counter the long term side effects of prolonged opioid use Each small pouch of powder sealed in unrecyclable plastic Snip it open There's always a small collection of tablets at my bedside I am disabled and an improved quality of life is pushed popped out of plastic packaging each evening each morning 30 milligrams at a time Plastic that also isn't recyclable [WHAT IS CODEINE MADE OF?] I am half reluctant to know what refined substances I have committed to in a state of reliance Named after the Ancient Greek κώδεια meaning 'poppy head' I have a poppy head I am a poppy head I have a head full of poppies The flowers placed in wreath pinned on shirts in remembrance The seeds which devastated South East Asia in the 1850s displaced millions of Chinese the First Opium War of 1839 – 1842 the Second Opium War of 1856 – 1860 encouraged in Singapore by the British colonial government as it reaped profit from opium licenses I'm unable to distance myself from being intimately bound up with these violences *Codeine can be extracted directly from the plant, most codeine is synthesized from the much more abundant morphine found in opium poppies* Last month the manufacturer changed from Teva UK Limited to Crescent Pharma Ltd From the*leading provider of medicines to the NHS* To one that *covers therapeutic areas* including antibiotics anticoagulants and painkillers The next day I add 'crip' to my Word dictionary I go back into London on October 15th extinction rebellion have been

banned from rebelling in London I am an hour early I
sit in a Pret near the river "Do you want it, it's free?" I
don't know his name he offers Lovingly Handmade Pret
Bar Full Of Fruit Goodness *This bar is full of goodness*
It goes off today I accept the moralism in flapjack
form No time or energy to eat before the seminar I
am complicit within the single use plastic economy
as I refuse food waste I am alone accompanied by Oh
Wonder's single Hallelujah *I heard it on the radio on my
way back home* I lip sync each word and evoke praise
and thanks for my continued being Inquiring to who
Each act of divine Briony There I made the reference
it made me happy too I am communal I will have to fly
by plane just before the new year I start helping out
in my parent's garden They grow tomatoes carrots
aubergines edamame garlic courgettes squashes
apples figs I will never be able to carbon offset the

footprint I will make have made I look into accommodation at the university I won't have a kitchen When I cook here I get to be vegan That won't be possible anymore To write about travel as a form of ecological movement across recycled material I travel into London and sit in a room of medics and think about contested interdisciplinary boundaries They talk about medical humanities as humanities belonging to medicine I long for I look for contemporary experimental poetics in every room I enter to retain an elusive formation of identity I will change I know I hope I will be kind A few weeks later I will hear someone say "We separate the disciplines so that we can be interdisciplinary" Perhaps writing in the space over British Rail lines is a form of palimpsestic oversite writing a mind the gap over sight response writing I am notified about my first academic interview 23 hours before it's due

Tied to the wind

31/08/2021

Afric McGlinchey

A death in the playground

Lusaka, Zambia. I have three friends at my new school. Anna and Gabi, both Italian, are only five-and-a-half. Anna has specs with big frames and a chocolate beauty spot to the right of her mouth, which God added like a full stop. Gabi is short-haired, a tomboy with a loud Nepalese accent. Maggie is a tumble of dark curls and *giddy*, her mum says. She has to be my number one friend because she's Irish and nearly-six, like me.

Maggie and Anna do the clapping in slow-motion to show me the pattern: *A sailor went to sea sea sea...*and the blue sea arrives in my head with a horizontal swoosh. A big feeling of emptiness follows. I miss Galway, the whooshing ocean practically at our front door. As I watch their flickering hands, I stumble back against a potting table, and the scent of its cedar wood pricks my nostrils and I fly

high up to the galley in the cathedral in Letterkenny, my aunt playing the organ, the choir singing, white incense trembling up like a nervous genie, and I'm leaning over the galley railing to look at all the lit candles far below and...

crash! An upturned red clay pot at the edge of the potting table tumbles to the floor, uncovering a coiled garden hose. Only it isn't a hose.

Near the open door, Maggie screams and flees, the other two scrambling after her. But I stand still as a tree, the snake only a few inches from my chest. It is acid green with black markings, rearing up like the letter Z we've just been practising in class, forked tongue flickering from its open jaw. The caretaker rushes in. He lifts a spade, twists it edgewise, then hammers down. As the spade finally slices through the muscular rope of the snake's body, the head falls to the dusty wooden floor. *A boomslang. One bite and you can be dead in twenty minutes...*his growly voice, one hand at the back of my head as he ushers me out.

It might have slept for months and then just slipped away without hurting anybody. But I toppled the pot. And now it's dead, and Maggie says her *amai* says that means I'll have bad luck for seven years.

Stinging insects and words

Kabwe, Zambia. I go round the side of the house and squat to pee, my knickers pulled down between my knees, feet apart, so I don't wet them. Force my pee fast, feeling sure someone's behind me, staring at my bum.

The someone is a mosquito. Smack!

As the sun droops redly into bed, insect sounds intensify. I swat at squads of mosquitoes trying to stand on my skin to gorge on my blood. Two victories, splats of brown-red, on the concrete.

Bedtime. Shrouded by the bliss of my cool, water-sprayed net, I'm misted into the universe of Neverland. Pause to take a few sips of water and hear the world again. A lift of breeze bangs the screen door. Birds chip the air, or maybe into wood. Another bang. Mum and Dad are having a drink on the verandah, outside my window. Just a little longer, my father says in a low voice. I hear him shove something up against the screen door. One of his boots, maybe. We'll be moving soon, he says.

And I'm the door, feeling the boot shoved into my mouth. The tree, feeling the stab of a bird's beak.

Rag in a gale

the wind, tearing
tiny tears from you
and making
your nose run
as you slap
against the sky
so hard
your body goes
high alert,
a bush warning.
That single,
off-kilter
step – into
nothingness.

To name a place is to manifest it

Dry, crackling, yellow *vlei*, east and west of us. Dad turns on the radio. Joy Cameron-Dow is giving the road report. *On the route from Salisbury North towards Kariba, road shoulders are being tarred...* Dad consistently reminds me about Ireland's endless rawky dampness. *Darwendale... Salisbury to Darwin...Gatuma the Que Que Road...*the cold so cold it feels alive, stabbing legs and cheeks, pinching fingers and toes, biting your teeth at the root. *Gwelo...Bulawayo...Victoria Falls...Beitbridge...* The summer wind so sharp and brisk, it strips the clouds into ribbons, erases the pale heat of a weak sun. *Marandellas...Headlands...Rusape... Inyazura.*

But Joy Cameron-Dow's blend of colonial and RP has me missing the lilt of Irish accents. Those weathers that would weave in and out endlessly, full of mystical, lit-up surprises. Those slow autumn days with misty beginnings. Maybe what I'm homesick for most is that sack of familiarity that I had managed to fill: expressions, soft weather, green world, the ocean, winding roads and the hills. The feeling of safety. *West Nicholson...Plumtree...Eastern Inyanga...Ruwa, Melfort, Bromley...*

Limerick, I think: *Galway, Dingle, Westport, Rutland, Gortahork, Letterkenny, Rathmullan, Derry, Dublin, Kerry, Wicklow, Cork.* Sometimes feel as though my *real* life is going on thousands of miles across the water, without me, while I'm on pause here.

Hollow

My fault. I was the one who urged her to leave. Not me though, Mum. Not leave *me.*

Ice-bucket tongs, one edge sharp as a mother who's left. Pressing into my palms, spindly marks. Light trickles down through the drooping willow leaves.

Owowowow! Blood from the brambles.

Ivor has gone. Mum has gone. Molly has gone.

His inability to resist the usual vultures, vodka bottles, sliced lemons. The usual ructions hammering through the wall.

I scrape at the ground. All the unrealised expressions of love, replaced by spikes, ignorings, hurtful sayings, missings. In the dirt, I doodle patterns. A skeleton of impressions.

You have your exams, she'd said. You need to stay. And look after your father.

For those three days, I didn't forgive her.

Study. Write exams. Study. Write exams. Study. Write exams. Study. Write exams.

Soon, it's all be over, and I'll be gone too.

Tear and share

31/08/2021

Leia Butler

Pick your path

Imagine the coldest, clearest distance,

Serrated   edges
separating

you

                     and what you've always wanted.

Numbers disguised by air's invisible ruler.

                     Concealed counting,

doubting,

     hidden in plain sight.

ı could go 2 meters forwards
ere its still like lukewarm tea,
    not yet close enough to feel the far.
    Just out of reach and
ıcing in the distance,
    laughing eyes disguise,
nows close is your safety blanket.
you step back
    and just watch it,
        regret better than risk

You could go 5 meters forwards
into cold cruel,
       bitter and blue,
but you can no longer just see it,
you've got it between icy fingers
       and pink cheeks,
and you drink it warm and welcoming like
its honey and lemon,
     tasting how it feels to win.

Nospaceforspace

so
letmein
I'lldrawmyselftoyou
likeawetwooljumper
aheavymattedhug
nospaceforspace
theairsmellslikemothsandmust
breathingisoverrated
itsreallytouchyouneedtosurvive
ahothandoveryourmouth
fireinyourface
meltingustomagnets

so you   say   you   need   space   for   spac•
        snagging   the   stitches   with   one   swift   sni|
                drawing   back   -   breathing   ice   ai

                        you   turn   us   to   negative•
                                cutting   the   connectio•

202

Forever small

How does it feel to be big?
 To crush people like peas
  / use buildings as building blocks
  /splashing in ocean puddles
   /toying with aeroplanes.

Big enough to leave someone small,
        so they'll forever be small
               and know only small
  Looking up to see a sky full of sole,
          every other step, a flash of blue,
  then back to dark dirt and clouds of gum.

And you walk on, littering your giant footprint,
           the small crawling in the mud moulds left behind.

Forget me not

Forgotten what it's like,
                              to see a stranger smile
full picture projections,

        or smell anything other than my own breath
        tinged with lucozade and loneliness.

    To touch skin not screens,
                greetings through glass,

        or taste air not tainted by bitter
            words flavoured with what ifs.

            To hear happiness,
                not having to rely on digital delight,

            senses deprived by having to be sensible
                    but far won't last forever.

Until Monday hits Sunday

Stay away

until A is so far from B it couldn't catch up if it tried

until you breathe all the way in,
    and it feels sharper than a fresh pencil
and so far out
       you fall apart

until the 30hr candle that smells of vanilla
          burns out into hot holly.

until its cold you can't see how it will ever be warm again
    and you only breathe in clouds.

Stay away
    until Monday hits Sunday and everything in between.

Breathe until you've filled up a pink balloon with tired air,
and stay away
       until you can no longer see it floating in the distance.

Blame it on Me

31/08/2021

Briony Collins

Harbour

I miss her smell – sand & tobacco,
wool & sea salt, sweetness of moss –
all the notes of my mother's body.

I miss her fingers – each shoreline
of her skin met with a crescent
bay of dirt she treasured there.

I miss her arms – a harbour opening,
a safe place for me to wreck myself
against the glaciers of growing up –

the way I craved them to hold me
on the morning she left herself,
no longer my marina,
but as blue as the sea.

Sunset

All you ask for on your last Earth night is a glass of water.
I hope you know what it really means – life thirsts to fill you.

Stay with me. Please.

How the skin cracks around your eyes, blackening with
the slow dilation of forever. How the milk of your bones

pours and empties, drowns you from the inside out.
How brittle you become in the pallid echoes of moonlight.

Don't go. Not just yet.

There is so much of this world left to share together:
how we will go to Rome and stand at the feet of Gods,

Hadrian's Venus, Saturnalia until sunset, Jupiter burning.
The depth of history you will miss as you cascade into it.

How at Ostia Antica we dream of long-dead stars reviving in
the amphitheatre, chips of stonework, ovation of ghosts.

Applause and awake.

All you ask for on your last Earth night is a glass of water.

Jasmine

Rain. How she was Jasmine and I was Briony, both named for plants and thirsting for a downpour in the same way, our skin bruised from playing hide-and-seek between the old caravans, some attached to cars and others propped on piles of bricks – the perfect picture of mortality: my best friend and me, five years old and giggling, next to their splintered remains.

Rain. How we sang in it before we'd heard of Gene Kelly or Nick Lucas, who found whispers of themselves decades beyond their voices in the off-beat trills of children who knew the words but not the melody. Somehow we made our warbling work, spinning an umbrella each like showgirls, not knowing where we learned those moves, only that they were ours and we were theirs.

Rain. How our fathers rigged up the festival swing boats together and saved us the red one at the end – bare-breasted women painted on each side so the drops ran down them like sweat and we understood that our bodies would become like theirs one day, but not today. Today we were pirates and a gale swept us through the seas of our song, living our childhoods for the first time, for the only time.

Comet

I'm the most delicate comet
to ever succumb to gravity.

I've been untethered
from my place in space,

watching the Earth breathe
underneath my body

as the floor rises –
dips its head in for a kiss.

The green carpet blurs,
softens in my aviation

so I can't see the stains
of food and wax and time.

The voile in the window
whispers in the vibrations

of the air, dances against
the lull of the city outside,

smiles yellow from smoke
of old cigarettes and grey

along the ends; feathers
of dusty osculation.

Blue walls spin across
the movement of vision,

remind me of the way
the sky looks on postcards.

I tell myself to smile –
it's only a game, only a game

my father plays. He doesn't
want to hurt me, even when

he sends me soaring
across the living room.

I'm a single, solitary rock
inbound for the sofa,

which catches me in its
cushions and cuddles me

close to stop me shaking.
I'm the most delicate comet,

still learning to live
with the trepidation

of elegant flight,
of poised fright,

curtain fall,
star fall,

the grace
of fear.

The Sound of Waking

Mornings are supposed to be lively:
        coffee beans, chaffinches, streams of
laughter caught in wind chimes.
        When you live alone they are silent:
you hunt patterns in the uneven ceiling
        paint while the weight of your skin
squeezes you between unwashed sheets.
        You attach yourself to your bed like
biofilm, tongue running over teeth, hands
        twisting the duvet tighter, a pillow
nothing but a nest for sebum and saliva.
        A dead arm lolls beside the body.

Sounds begin to creep, mingle together
        with the tinnitus of loneliness,
the first signs that you are starting to wake.
        The jackdaws outside beg each other,
remind you to check your social media
        for the same noise – thousands of
people echoing their own names: *jack, jack,*
        jack, from behind a glass parting.
There must be one thing – *one thing –*
        to get up for today
                (pick at that thought like a day-old scab,
                    tender and ripe for another blood-letting).

Who would notice if you stayed in bed
        and fantasised about dark passages,
the damp earth, eulogies?

repeating mouths

31/08/2021

Adrienne Wilkinson

fish eye

it was there that i saw it
on the bed
among the stains and the tangles of cloth
before a fisher caught my attention
trawling his slow groans over the sheets
longing
like sad trumpets

it was there
a moving thing
like when you took me to the museum and you showed me
the pubescent tadpole
the fish with legs
whose tiny limbs pressed against the glass
which it struggled to climb

as we watched
you told me about the mermaid with a fish head and human legs
what kind of sailors did she catch? with flat eyes
and big O mouth
breathing saltwater

yes it was there
on the tangles of cloth
in the tank
yes
where i   all gills   lay

biting the head off a worm

we are sitting at the same table
we are talking in the same language

when i open my mouth who knows what will come out
everything changes with touch

the grass / the dirt
me / you

the soft and eager earthworm moves with its whole body
you feel the mulch of it between your toes

sinew / viscous
soil soil soil

the water wash tenders skin
the sugar scrub the mud
the peel of acid
against worm flesh

you watch it all
feeding gently from the root
growing where you water it

you as a mole

or molehill
dirt under your nails
star nosed
all the worms you've been eating

you in a small
tunnel
through the dark
you through the dark
grubbing

my feet either side of the molehill
something different used to grow here

as you work
the soft dirt does strange things
to your mole hands
which fall
in fleshy clumps
through the ground

ragwort

you step in and lay your body on the unmarked space
you will be entered here
and   here
the helpful woman says the word
                                        uncomfortable

table legged   you are
open   you are
and the white of the stomach meets
the light of the operating theatre
knife handled you   are moved
from consciousness into another
time   darkened   space

do you remember the first time you had sex
your knickers graze the moon as they wash down the river
a rubbing of an eclipse
the wet of the log dug into your back

do you remember when they pushed it in   the needle

that's my blood!
that's my womb!

you come across a plant covered in black and yellow caterpillars
they live on the plant because it is poisonous
it is your job to pull the plant up

you are guilty as a scorpio
blood-handed

the limpness of supple leaves and you ragged
the white of the stomach below meeting
that dog-handled space

lamp lit ritual of our courtship

me & you crouched
in the alleyway
peeing

watching
our lines
interlace:

bouncing light
and dark
between the pebbles

The Rosebud Variations

30/09/2021

Jaydn DeWald

Past Developing

Forget the waitress who resembled Sappho.

Between the tines of our forks. On the tube

But even that light made her cheeks glisten.

And raised the centuries-old wine that had

Suit I wore in college—the darkness inside.

To which Odysseus had been tied. And yet

Via video surveillance. Our hunk of peasant

We carried around our necks huge Polaroid

Through red window curtains, light caught

On the specials chalkboard, the old barman

The salt cod she served us drifted like sand

Sat children painting little clay St. Jeromes,

"I'm greener than the grass is green," I said,

Our heads spinning. I dreamt of the Gorilla

Behind the bar stood the rotted, black mast

Its placard: *None of this is being preserved*

Bread. Those paper placemats. Plates of oil.

Cameras, so there was no use remembering.

Us red-handed, napkins rising to our noses.

Playing Hangman. One leg. No I's. No face.

Round Midnight

Back seat of a train car   the black water rush
Of night   outside the windows   watching you
Pick your cuticles   over a battered blue-
And-yellow paperback   *On Meditation*
As you in a whisper   almost a hiss   explain
That for us to have remained   that static-misty winter
Together   would have   like an animal
Like a frenzied creature   shoved again and
Again into its dirt tunnel   killed you
That was why   I arrived home mid-   afternoon
Cloudlight through sheer curtains   barges
Lowing in the bay   to a bedroom pillaged
A few crumpled garments   sweat-grayed panties
On the floor   and now   slowly from your fore-
Finger   a beadlet of blood   falls
Onto the book cover   which you instantly
Wipe   with your green knit scarf and at which
Years later   I will gaze   sliding the slim volume
From our shelf   in the shadow-latticed hall
A faint russet streak   I will press
To the tip of my tongue   the way one
Tests a battery   for tingling   and still I am
Here beside you   in the flickering
Fluorescent train lights   like a man lost
Inside a monstrous costume   watching his hands
Unbodied   through two   too distant eye-
Holes   sweep strands of hair from
Your forehead   so that I   without touching you
Can touch you   pull you   against my chest
That shared wall   thick with damp fur
Inside me   on the other side of which I eaves-
Drop on my own life   and on you
Verily gasping out   a volley of apologies
Into the heart   of my liver-   purple sweater
Though my propensity   for silent reflection
For standing   unblinking   at the kitchen sink

Just holding a grease-smeared enamel plate   and remembering
Some childhood   morning with its blond light
Lighting the blond hair   of my inner thighs
As "Round Mid-   night" crackled on the turntable
Must have contributed   to your leaving
To your deep   zero-gravity sleep in some-
Body else's red cotton sheets   dreaming of insects
I want to believe   when in fact you'd told me
Already   over lattes and burnt pancakes
In shabby Empire chairs   that in those three
Soft-focus months with-   out me
You had become less a person   than a thing
A body of wind   sewn   into the very air
A dream   of invisibility   and so
I stand suddenly   like the captain of a ship
In the bow   riding the black river   of night
And yank the bell cord   because this is our
Stop   and we need to walk   home together
Arm in   arm against the cold-wet   wind
I   the husband   you need me
To pretend to be   leading us down the train's steps
And out into darkness   the orange-brown
Pools of street-   lamps *On Meditation*
Slipped in my left rear   trouser pocket   a coward-
Hero   still silent   still unblinking
Taking your chewed-up   finger into my mouth

Voyage Out

He's standing beside his hammock, above his sleeping body, which dreams of stumbling along an ever-winding path of leaves & ashes, when a distant, quavering soprano begins to sing—a voice he'd heard, years before, on a bronze hill overlooking the ocean, & ever since regretted not searching for, not hurtling toward her in the rubescent dusk of summer, tearing off his rucksack. "Wake up," he tells his body, nudging its shoulder with his knee. But it goes on lying there, like an enormous baby in a sling, because it is dying in its sleep: it has collapsed on the dark path among the scraping leaves, watching his twelve-year-old daughter in her plum-black dress (so like a dream within a dream) stumble forward in its place. He runs his hand over the blond hairs of its forearm. Then he stares up at the white light through the lemon trees & at his daughter dancing, one rainy evening, before the old projector, the old faces of relatives (contorted, celery-green) streaked across her flannel PJs. What can account for this desire to hurtle out into the streets, to find the soprano's voice, rising again, in the paling distance? *Art thou a little spirit bearing up a corpse,* as Epictetus said, or is the soprano tempting him—like an egret on a thin branch—to leave, to let the body go? His daughter, at the beach with some friends, in the tarantualic shadow of a palm tree, will no doubt walk, hours later, over the damp grass toward his body, then suddenly freeze in the middle of the yard—warm & windless & the moon in her salt-hardened hair—noticing a smudge of white, the peak of his nose, above the hammock. Now he's touching for the last time (as his daughter will, crumpling to her knees) the paper eyelids, the colorless lips & ill-shaven chin. O how he's dreamt of the soprano silhouetted on an ice floe, of lurching toward her through rags of swirling snow, burning to see her, to watch her sing! Soon his daughter, as she replaced his body in its dream, will be standing right here in this place before the hammock, trying again & again to shape these wooden fingers around her tiny hand— although by then, of course, he will be long gone, loping across violet sands, searching for the soprano: the quavering voice, the painted mouth . . .

Landscape with Martyr

Afterward, he watched her lumber out of the coliseum
Swinging the severed head of his panther—

All that talk about Madrid and his old Segovia albums
And look what good it did them. Outside,

In the pomegranate dusk, she flung the panther's head
Into the sidecar of her sepia '57 Triumph

And roared, her orange hair flapping, into the distance.
Remember the mirror over their pine bed

In Ohio, loving her double nakedness night after night
With the snow falling? His mind escaped

Into that fragrant, still-warm profusion of white sheets
And denied (kissing her ears) the present

Wherein he stood at the ironwork gate of the coliseum
Watching her panther's tail of black dust

Settle over the stone field. (Touching her arched spine,
Listening to the fizzle of the phonograph

In the static winter dark.) Later, restored to the present,
He would lug his headless cat to a furrier

And make of it a coat, luxurious, with abalone buttons;
In the meantime, he alternated his mouth

Between one tamarind nipple and the other, expecting
A little talk, afterward, about the beaches

Outside Valencia. *Ribbons of spume in the lapis water,*
Clam boats pitching in the diamond light—

Then he watched, in real time again, her Triumph melt
Into the mercurial horizon. It was crucial,

He felt, to attend the final scene. Raising his right arm,
He told the spectators to go home. Listen

To Segovia. Eat dinner. Keep your roses to yourselves.

Littoral Couplets

first sweat
  then glitter

beneath her
  i was an orb

of vapor slow-
  dissolving

bari sax
  for sunrise

double bass for
  humid nights

she wailed
  across the moon-

lit waters
  like a ship

once
  in a salt cave

i licked
  a wall until my

tongue bled
  the dawn rose

at the nape
  of her neck

later
  in the crushed

mica
  on my chest

she traced
  a cabin

hum for me
  she whispered

the ballad
  on the gramo-

phone inside
  often then

i sensed her
  in darkness

sheared my
  white hair

the shore's scent
  the ship's wail

i hurled my
  shadow upon

her shadow
  in the sand

Collected Experimentalisms: 1997-2000

30/09/2021

U. G. Világos

Remember your experience.

I was sent to the army and was suspected to have died.

I am lying in the face of Jesus Christ.

If you're wasting away, do so in the city of books.

I want to know that the game is standing on its wall and it's a level bleeding system.

You can talk to me at any time.

Dreams come true but are they great?.

The goal is to reach people on the Internet, to draw a new cat with ropes and thorns.

Sorry, I want to create something more interesting than fun.

I placed a pillow next to me and saw myself move into a new apartment.

This is the best way to get rid of dust and debris, I call it 'a library'.

'What a great way to meet at night.'

I cannot see myself, my friend.

When the contract is completed, the author ceases to care for their own maintenance.

I want to be a whole band, or to be a movie star.

(Rattle before you read the last part of this book).

I come back, time & again, to my own self-deprecation.

I heard love as a chant at a football game.

I tried everything and I couldn't find my will to live.

My father not only thinks that I am only half human but he also thinks that this is one of the few books I have written by myself, without the call of spirits.

I tried having internal night-time keto.

I saw heaven only under luminous discotheques.

Reading every thing I've rated exceptional.

Forests read on music, plants over every thing resting yesterday.

God is not like God.

Actually Dad, thanks for reading, it was good for me.

Looks like PDF code, PDF code, PDF box, jelly or brick.

I think it's like a brick, a brick of a brick.

Colors and style make me laugh.

I slept in the director's room and played music, lighting, eggs, coffee.

I was a bottle, and a cup of olives and ice typing.

Make sure there are no air bubbles or clear weights.

Check out my new genetic makeup.

That's my face, okay, but hide it.

Every testimony of mine is better than the gospel of the Bible.

This warms my heart

This is an amazing point in the book.

He must decide what the pizza is covered with and proceed to sell the swaggle with the dog.

Am I dead or merely in the other two seas?

Depending on the screen and the rules, spots may appear on both wrists at the same time.

Other features include: soil drying and forever dying.

Within five seconds, add salt & grass.

My mother is fine, but I am not.

My body warms up when you touch the window.

Yes, you may shake hands with the table.

'You can trust us'.

The fourth method of all periclitavants (except SCG) is dry ice.

This book contains 6 decorative spices.

They come to us, fly at night, catch trains, drink the doppler effect by heart, basil, and move like shadows.

After reading this book, after looking at it, when I read the original book again, I think that I should not read the story anymore.

Captain King did not play his first game in Canada last month.

This month we are in Ellis, USA; where the Gods live.

We can't measure Gods, only idols.

The first thing I did was to report the pain.

There was a problem with the pain.

Doctor, I see you as a biological father.

(He rejected it).

He closed his eyes and I entered a safety net.

Will you smile and compliment me when we dance, doctor?

I'm stuck with false father figures forever.

Another problem associated with headaches is severe illness.

I am often heavy and unreliable which adds strength, beauty, and invisibility.

Anger at karaoke is not due to the introduction of people, languages, children, and the general public.

Everything is perfect.

When I talk about this book I'll present it with pictures of Velcro.

Not or the first time I started laughing, the other children looked at me, laughed and applauded, and stopped punishing me - I think they saw me as human for the first time.

Today she is wearing a bright red dress from the south, socks with straps and a blue apple that reflects the marriage we couldn't save.

Everything is perfect.

We're closing the gap.

Here are some suggestions on how to seek treatment for your child: do, seek it, seek treatment.

Even though I didn't feel anything, he walked my helpless hands, covered my mouth and my blue eyes, and told everyone that the ball was out of the water.

I must find food.

As a last resort, I threw my soul into a first-aid kit and sent it in a box with pictures of metals, alloys, and medals, so I was no longer unworthy of our secrecy.

But, I then prayed and put the box in the box.

I prayed for funeral services.

The only way to open my father's closet is to suffer.

The film continues.

Everything is perfect.

I will follow the spirit and feel the warmth of her dead wine, whose tongue of a white tree holds us in broken glass.

She jumped up and tossed the mailbox into the park near the road, the water, and the Red Sea.

As the sun set, clouds gathered in the sky and fish on their shores.

That is all.

So don't worry.

Fools are not allowed in caves.

Police shouted that no one was flying in the clouds.

They were very angry and threw themselves into a wooden box.

I've never met a cop I didn't hate.

I am not confused.

I have started something.

Covid/Corvid

30/09/2021

Alyson Hallett & Penelope Shuttle

3

drilling down the air to the sea   were you
is that what you were at   bishbashbosh
          no drill bit big enough to zero out
the pesky covid why's it so like corvid
clever buggers those birds   brain the size of a pea
                but they're more synaptically adjusted
than many a   toree toree toree   i'd a notion
the earth was a witch when i walked in the woods
          earlier   saw her stitching the virus
into a net and casting it out   like spray from
          a waterfall's mouth   a hoick of germs
on the back of a toad   you know how it goes
          one iceberg to us   a few hundred thousand
humans to the planet   for compost
          I'll show you   the earth might have said
vindictive   vendetta   oh what I'd give to be in a gondola
          skimming along as if   nothing was wrong

AH

12

fuck handwashing
fuck the sanitizer fuck the mask
fuck the gloves o ex-cuse me the fucking
fucking disposable gloves
fuck lockdown blues
fuck the fucking four walls closing in for fucks sake
fuck the supermarket queue   fuck the medical officers
fuck the cabinet the parliament our dozy crime minister
fuck washing the groceries in soapy water
fuck my outdoor shoes   fuck my indoor shoes
fuck my indoor clothes   my fucking outdoor garments
fuck the tories and fuck the fuck out of their fucking family trees
for ten generations past and for ten generations to come
in short   and let me make this perfectly clear   fuck

PS

1

Did that just happen?
                    Did a mason bee lay eggs in the hollow
metal tube in a chair on a balcony
then stuff it with moss? Did a government of
the twenty first century sanction driving sixty miles
to a castle and back as a way for their favourite
advisor to test if his eyes were working? Did the sky
strip itself of clouds for three whole weeks? Did I
dance in the Odd Down park-and-ride in a red dress,
did I walk in the middle of the road on white white
lines and live to tell the tale? Who is this haunting
the topsy-turvy screen? Some days I craved an ice-cream.
Some days I zoomed around the world. Some
days I knelt on the kitchen floor and wept with
the people in the radio as they buried their dead.

AH

8

&&
&&&
&&&&
&&&&&
or the horse
may snap
on this fine & dandy day
given the legacy
of empire
&&&&&
&&&&
&&&
&&
&

PS

12

there are about 70 billion of them somewhere
the dead of the world since the world began
with their 70 billion smiles or frowns
perhaps they can't bear to drift off into the void
perhaps they're long gone and that faint sighing you hear
in the middle of the night (no need for a Ouija board)
isn't the 70 billion singing to pass the time but just your ear for the spooky
    is there time or place for the 70 billion? (I'm not bothering
    with heaven or hell because *duh*…)
    we'll join the billions someday   there's no getting round it
    we'll be the holy ghosts of us
    the last vestige butterflying round the globe
    in our extinction dance   the biggest congregation
    this side of the mountains of the moon

PS

Writing through Siddhartha

30/09/2021

Andre Bagoo

a long detour
a long look
a long meditative recitation
a long path
a long pause
a long sequence
a long silence had occurred
a long time
a long time after midnight
a long time afterwards
a long time ago
a long time had yearned
a longing

his ardent will
his arms
his arms folded
his arms were hanging down
his beard
his breath
his business-deals
his chest
his companion
his counterpart
his course
his dormant spirit suddenly woke up
his entire body like the lukewarm
his entire long sleep had been nothing but
his eyes
his eyes became motionless
his eyes fixed
his eyes were fixed on
his eyes were rigidly focused towards
his eyes were starting
his face
his farewell
his fate
his father
his father appeared
his father felt
his father had said
his father's son
his fear
his fears flowed
his feet
his finger closed her eyelids
his forehead
his friend
his futile fight against them
his future is already
his gestures
His glance turned
his goal
His goal attracts him

Siddhartha also felt desire
Siddhartha also remembered everything
Siddhartha answered
Siddhartha asked his host
Siddhartha ate his own bread
Siddhartha awakened
Siddhartha began
Siddhartha bent down
Siddhartha bid his farewell
Siddhartha bowed with
Siddhartha can wait calmly
Siddhartha collapsed
Siddhartha continued
Siddhartha could
Siddhartha did
Siddhartha does
Siddhartha emerged
Siddhartha entered the chamber
Siddhartha even doubted
Siddhartha exclaimed
Siddhartha exposed himself
Siddhartha felt
Siddhartha felt his blood heating up
Siddhartha felt more
Siddhartha ferried across
Siddhartha found himself being dragged away
Siddhartha gave him
Siddhartha gave his garments
Siddhartha got
Siddhartha had
Siddhartha had also been hearing
Siddhartha had always watched
Siddhartha had assumed
Siddhartha had been partaking
Siddhartha had gotten into
Siddhartha had intended to
Siddhartha had learned
Siddhartha had lived the life
Siddhartha had spent the night
Siddhartha had started

flocked
flowed
flowers
flowing
fly
foamed
folded
follow

everything always becomes
everything came back
everything can be learned
everything could be
Everything else
everything enter his mind
everything has
everything has existence
everything is
everything is Brahman
everything is coming
everything is easy
Everything is one-sided which can be thought
everything is perfect
everything only
everything shown
everything was

Iarnród Éireann

30/09/2021

Simon Barraclough

Iarnród Éireann

The Spanish–Italian border was dismantled overnight
and the next day rusting flatbeds, snakes of freight,
metal fatigued as all fuck groaned into view, uncoiling wire,
pitching barriers, angle-grinding watchtowers and turrets
with migraine sparks, and the English–Nazi border was christened
with street parties of Rippers & Crippens & Mosleys & Haw-Haws.
My heart had long lapsed, too expensive to renew,
the biometrics broken down, but I had my mother's papers
and a code word she swaddled in lullabies now lost but not forgotten.
To Dublin, then! With McCabe the Assassin,
on one of the last helicopters out of Sigh Gone,
a DC-3 out of West Berlin, an old crate out of Silvertown,
wings and fuselage clogged by imperial sugar work,
a sticky crash-landing in the Liffey, doggy-paddling
down the Dodder till we found a wharf to gorge on Gorgonzola
with grinning green teeth and a bottle of Burgundy
from a sommelier who left no reflection
as the mirror-food floated towards us.

Fade to black with matt glasses of Vantablack® Guinness,
the most profound material known to man;
pints of vertical carbon nanotube
horizontally aligned by the end of the day;
a substance so dark it would razor off Narcissus's fizzog

and wear it to Carnivale; a liquid so dense
it sequesters a thousand millennia of shipwrecks
in a fleck of quantum foam; a gaze so unflinching
it could mine your deepest buried obscenities
and post them on the hymn board of every church in Ireland;
a drink so light-sapping your lips tingle with Hawking radiation
as you place the Kubrick monolith back onto the beermat.
And from its depths we conjured an extempore lament,
the gallows-dodging McCabe and I:

I hate it when people jump off the right bridge but land in the wrong river;
I hate it when people take money from other countries but sell their loan words;
I hate it when the power of Christ compels wrapping paper;
I hate it when you blanch at the thought of a feral hedgehog in the Languedoc;
I hate it when rapacious lyricists eulogise Yorkshire womanisers;
I hate it when people are devoted to pure, sky-fucking jouissance;
I hate it when men with wide ties don't share their sandwiches;
I hate it when people invoice me at midnight;
I hate it when your ten euro looks like a grilled rasher;
I hate it when people conflate a sausage crucifix with a breakfast get-out;
I hate it that Five Guys Named Moe on Grey Velvet *is not a giallo musical;*
I hate it when you send me your annual syntax bill;
I hate it when they say the sun's death will seal a trade deal with Proxima Centauri.
I hate it when the receipt number for ten Guinness is 13.

Deeper, then, sans McCabe, into the verdant vulvaland,
Iarnród Éireann from Dublino to Luimneach,
Intercity, a head full of Hell, INRI, Iron Nails Ran In,
with *Mercier and Camier* sharing my table,

all elbows and shanks, playing footsie with the sleepers,

buggering any gap with the bitching gab,

shuffling trips to the buffet car for miniatures

and sticking up the trolley for plasticated Jamesons.

What are trains but wormholes through weather?

What's a drinks trolley but a clattering CAT-scan

of your liver's livid inventory?

What are *Taytos* but body bags for tuber leprosy?

I tried to read but trainshake breeds flies from the alphabet,

juddering runes using sandwiches as treadmills,

vomiting the small print of the universe we never read

but still click **Agree**. Raindrops try to board

but have such small hands they can't carry tickets.

They clamp themselves to the gritty windows,

limpet mines triggered long-distance by light.

Light sleep broken by the brakes at Limerick Junction

where I grab somebody's bag and nearly alight

with a second life, a counterfeit self.

A good time to switch points, change the tune,

find a new electron shell to bat about above my crib.

Hitting 50 I'm fusing iron at the core,

can feel my organs turning over in their sleep,

hitting snooze on cell regeneration,

shouldering into flesh duvets to snatch an hour more.

My heart is scared to go out these days

for fear of who might be on the landing, on the stairs;

peeps through net curtains to see if the coast is clear.

It should be nailed beneath floorboards, telling tales

in the splintered dark with a murdered cat for company.
Maybe if I'd had children I would be braver of necessity?
My dad thought I was 'soft.' I just wanted to climb trees
and learn the constellations and stay above trouble.

Trolley-bag-lugging over the Shannon
I think of my grandfather tipping my mother
from a currach into the chill swell
for her first swimming lesson. Apocryphal?
Perhaps, but I hear her splash, taste the weed
reaching down her green throat and plucking
the strings from the harp of her lungs,
stuffing sheets of lost music into a strongbox
bound with chains and burying them in the silt
to choke and rust. The Salmon of Knowledge
lashed past her face, flicking a thin cicatrix
with a fin of foresight but she misread the sign,
took it for a grinning muddy pike and in the labour
of unwisdom dropped me into the world
on the old maternal Yoni yo-yo.
Bouncing the baggage into the Strand Hotel
I'm bumped up to 'the executive floor' and a croissant on my pillow,
a Corby trouser press for my tongue or lingam,
a life-coach crouching on the foot of the bed.
Awaken in the boot of a car coasting bumps
on the way to Woodcock Hill Bog for a team-building day
of trust games, foraging and grave-digging.
And then I'm really awake to Limerick rain tapping its metres
on business-class windows, straining for rhymes in the dusk.

On with leaky red shoes into monochrome drizzle

that falls like Anna Magnani onto neorealist rubble.

A writer buys shoes every five years and these Doc Martens

have split from the miles, evolving gills on their bellies;

flounders, bottom-feeders, sand-hiders, muggers of crabs and hermits.

All the sodden way to the house my mum was raised in,

pigeonhole for a hundred birthday cards, an address

hid to memory that the hand knows, the pen knows,

the ink imprints with platelets and plasma.

One Christmas I forgot to write it down but kissed

the envelope and the card found its way to my aunty's house.

What does Lacan say about letters always arriving?

He's an awful eejit! Sure he doesn't know us from the sky above us, like.

What has Lacan to do with the peaty smell in the air?

My first taste of foreign soil, my second whiff

of the womb's perfume on a Möbius litmus strip

of Anglo-Irish, Irish-English, the whole clan

branded with an unbreakable lineage of freckles,

future sunburns, fading stigmata that bleed under UV,

flash mob the forearms to simulate Mediterranean tans,

that once had me scrubbing my cheeks with a pumice stone

and bleach so no teacher could ever ask me again,

'Were you sunbathing under a sieve?' Well,

welcome Limerick rain, seep through my insoles,

anoint my feet, trickle your peaty vortices into the wounds.

The gravelly drive, the pebbly portico,

refuge for umbrellas in the porch behind jewelled glass.

I squelch into view, am greeted by my uncle's voice,

Speculum

31/10/2021

Hannah Copley

Speculum

According to James Marion Sims, "Father of Modern Gynaecology",
who wrote his life story in the imaginatively named *The Story
of My Life*, when another physician heard that he was heading
to doctor the Westcott plantation, he remarked:

> 'you had better take
> your instruments along with you,
> for you may want to use them'.

Let's place all the emphasis on the *want*,
given how quietly terrifying it is. *Murder,*

She Wrote is on the tv again and there has been
a gruesome death at the beach, but luckily
Jessica thought to pack rubber gloves, measuring
tape, notebook, pen and a Dictaphone
in her bag.

Hyperemesis Gravidarum

Ignore the Smirnoff Black balanced on a headstone   don't
take into account the whisky in a water bottle at lunchtime
labels can be picked off in longing   other people's butts get
re-born behind the garage   we're in the morning after the
night before and there is no water near the bed   and you
remember   the meat falling off the donner like a dress
     that *gluey pie*   all the wet throats   and it is *Dangerous
Liaisons: why syphilis   and gonorrhoea have returned to haunt
Britain*   while strangers push their tongues to the back of
your throat   the unwatered breath   but labels can be
picked off   in longing   don't sweat the muscular hollows
of your heart   or   a bad joke   and there's the saliva again
there's the raw pork in the pan   the foreskin facials on
Groupon   you chat briefly   to a co-worker
about water boarding before going back   to your desk
the school pays a visit to the abattoir   is it still
there rotting in the fridge   you're a yellow streak   of piss
the bin smell on a Thursday   and I'm   all nosegays
and chewing gum and ginger   and I'm going to brush
your teeth again   it is swilling   it is swallowing   it is
owning up it is queasy   I'm practicing   all the words
like bilious   and viscera   and qualms   and burdens
for the smell of his body   because sometimes labels can be
picked off skin   it is his turn this time   it is your body
it is all in your belly   it is all in your womb   it is all in
your mind   it is all in your mouth.

Person of the Year
[three hours]
I.M. Salomé Karwah. 1988 – 2017.

Ye   a'a   but   struggling to   you through the   [as
in partition - as in lover wrapped tight in a thin sheet – as in heavy
rains on tin] Stay   car, ma   m [as in passage – as in tin can
cracked earthen - as in any other jar to hold each piece of grief]
Don't   yourself [as in to fret is to be alive] Today is   day
for us   [as in the sound the road makes when it
melts] No, glass   necessary [as in water as in bread as in touch is
not] An absolute [as in there should be a thing other than
absolutes] No,   is   on call   [as real as you or I
or Jesus Christ barely an idea in the mind of his mother]
glove is esse   al [as a road is – as a light]   mask is
essential too [as a cracked tap is – as a wing shorn bird still flaps]
you can   I'm also hot [as the sun is sometimes burnt by
itself] But I can't   through all   glass [as in father in a
thin sheet in a burning box] No ma'am,   stay [as in I cannot
hold even the coil of a shed hair] Lie yourself   the
seats [as in a makeshift tent unfurls] No, don't roll it   [as
in the stink   of hazmat sweat – as in the human smell of rot]
I can't   it hurts   [as in bad womb stitch bad
split – bad mouth - as in how blood and spit don't know
themselves - as in bad scratch - as in odour as in wound - as in red
cross like the sun's own – as in each tethered spot of grief] Not
t   ching   essential [as in all absolute things are] you remain
import   us [as in feared – as in unmade – as in a living
object] plea   don't r   down   ndow [as in I will never
carry you   away from this place] There is no
  one

Now, Suture

         leaves scars
smooth and neat like cable wire,
so the laddered track above your left wrist
betrays your age
                 (as does the way
the skin now has a memory of its own,
crêpeing when pinched only to fall away).
I run my finger to where the purple line
has bunched,
           and feel silk snagged
in the two - pronged foot of the machine.

Its pucker,
        and the way the corners itch
when it's about to snow
               (think of
the ache of a phantom leg,
             or the herd
of cows that lie and wait upon their bellies
as the pressure falls)
           says nothing
of what witchcraft might have hemmed
the pieces of your skin and bone
back together,
        or what tore them
open first.

        Prizing old wounds apart,
I glimpse your body in free fall,
            poised
between the garage roof and concrete floor:
the slow-motion playback of your radius,
jaunty,
     sharp,
        as it breaks free from the bicep
and pierces a new window through
the epidermis;
        hear the brittle crunch
of bone as it shatters.

Although we can
all marvel at the durability of children,
there must still be a sort of poignancy
in a trepanned arm,
                    a sadness held
in fingers that for two long hours
don't listen when they're told to bend.
I flinch to think of the cut telephone cord
and its fiddly re-wiring.
                         The tentative
current creeping,
                  then coursing
between your hand and the bundle of threads
tucked just beneath your skull.

It's only a playful trick though,
                                 this little leap
between what's fact and what's pulled
out of the hat
               (I hardly look down
when I pick you up.)
                    and with luck
it'll be my arms
                 - almost as thin as yours -
searched for ugly marks.
                         Besides,
 it's always only the capacity of a verb
to crack,
          smash,
                  splinter,
                            and then recast
that's really at stake.

Emily Dickinson keeps writing me love letters

with tiny black peonies where each tittle should be
and exclamation marks at the end of every other sentence.

I am so excited! I am so sad! Emily Dickinson keeps declaring.
She writes long passages about the varying properties of roots

and then follows it with things like *my heart is made* —
of ringing bells and *we are a basket of herbs bound tight*

in God's twine! and I don't know what to think.
And all the while the dogs are outside

barking to be let back in and it hasn't stopped raining
in seventeen days. Each time I go to look up oscillation

another dried sprig falls out of the dictionary, and I remember
just how long there still is to go. Last week, when I opened

the kitchen window at least thirteen dead ladybirds fell
onto my hand, and if that isn't a sign then I don't know what is.

Balanuve

31/10/2021

Poems: Gregory Leadbetter
Photography: Phil Thomson

The Damage

The city's defences –
nothing more than railings,
plucked up by their stone roots
are junk: rows of surrendered spears.
It didn't take a battle to break
everything – leave the city empty tins
of beer and Spam like detonated IEDs
next to a child's scooter – cardboard boxes
fit for heroes. The air is paste
at fifty yards – allotments filled with chemical
rubble. A spike runs through a rag
of clothes. A petrol can has been drunk dry,
mistook for water – North Sea Oil
mistook for a future. This slew of wrack
is the coughed-up spoil of the century –
a few million lifetimes left to corrode.
Dumped like this, a heap of random
sweepings – raw material. When you arrive,
pick your way to the centre. Look –
a wheel. It will have to be reinvented.

Levitation

The children are playing again
and one little girl is levitating:
what looks like the sling of a skipping
rope is the unlikely bow of her levity.
She holds out her arms, grips
what could be maracas or electrodes,
lifts her feet and off she goes.
Her friends are entirely unfazed:
it's just a thing you do at playtime.
A girl in a bobble hat waits her turn
but she better cheer up: you have to
feel something like joy to levitate.
Like salmon returning to native rivers
playground levitation is a good sign:
for once, they are doing something right.
The school could do with some planting
but it looks pretty clean: those spots
of blood will wash with the rain.
Remember, children, when levitating:
bad thoughts bring you down again.

Cathedral

The city has a recurring dream.
Gates fit for Babylon open
on a depot the size of
a cathedral. Skylights
beam through a vaulted roof,
illuminate fumes like incense
from the last running engine.
Buses that will never leave
are housed like giant cattle
in their shed, fattened
for the abattoir. It is not clear
if this is the beginning
or the end, but it is somehow
the centre of the world.
There is a man in a buttoned-up
uniform, dwarfed by the place
but officious as a bishop
in his church. He is dipped
in shadow. He may not know
his part in all that's gone
before, all there is to come.
He has the look of one
who does a good job, then
heads for home, untroubled
by the epic scale of what
surrounds him, nor the facts
that find and make him.
There's innocence in that,
perhaps, but in the dream it is
unwary. The city mutters
in its sleep. Every night
he walks towards a black
hole he has not seen. The city
wakes: another dawn.

Bad Sermons

31/10/2021

Luke Kennard

1

'I see what's happened here.'

We were driving into this driving rain

She climbed under the table and carefully lifted each leg in turn, picking out and brushing away a dusty piece of corrugated cardboard under the first, a torn beermat from under the second and an old wad of tissue from under the third.

I waited as I always do.

'I don't love you.'

A fire door marked Hotel.

'I can be happy.'

We've started now, haven't we? In all honesty.

This isn't a door: there's nothing behind it.

2

They lacked plot, certainly, and in some cases dialogue, but character was rarely the issue.
Fumbling with the top button of her jeans.

Hard not to regress when surrounded.

The rope snicked in the buckles.

Certainly there were families … references to their own mythology.

'Do you remember?'

the garden had "returned to nature",

took this as evidence of why he'd left
rather than what he'd done to her

well well well more than one thing can be true
which is both objectively real and…

is this the way to hell?

way?!

Pal.

'Oh yeah.'

Tara said very little on the hour's drive back,

the empty mug in the foot-well of the passenger seat.

I think we pass for normal,

prone to spending whole days at the black plastic edifice—

3

a static caravan crossed with a check-in booth
The only lunch an artist should eat;

A bowl of grass.

a static caravan crossed with a check-in booth

a tremendous beard and a disconcertingly gamey smell.

no indication that she was especially bothered by any of the above

so not to worry.

Temporarily dismissing him from the office

I went to fetch glasses,

A vase of water too beautiful, heavy and ungainly to pick up,

entertaining a visiting dignitary.

The most disingenuous man who ever lived.

constant encouragement

'This is different,' she said.

ordered a lager top from a girl with red cherry earrings.

A little too easily.

'No they don't.'

Anxious journalists and intellectuals huddled.

'Just pick a critical apparatus.'

Across the sandy path like an injured but determined bear.

Like an injured but determined bear across the sandy path.

'Not busy?'

'Actually I wanted to say thank you.'

Thank you. I don't mean any of this, but it's nice.

The pond where a mallard appeared had disappeared.

4

Blessed is the

obtrusively loud clock

an American child.

An entire culture based around being happy for people.

Her mother once admonished her for this,

another weekend of suspect houseguests

amazed to be somewhere with a view.

He seemed to be interested in everything.

I need to get out of this country.

I'm sick. You have to believe me. You have to forgive me.

You have to do no such thing.

Inheritors of a difficult situation.

They sat on high stools at the counter and read together:

forget, if you can, your favours and that right which they claim over me;

To look through the clouded glass and see the doorway at the back of the shop,

so at first she didn't realise that the customer clambering towards her…

5

She *saw* herself.

What will I do without you

What are we going to do with you

like a lavish gift

after the plenary

'Very bad for you.'

As if the balcony

in his experience,

shivering, as if the balcony

of his experience creaked.

Spoil

31/10/2021

Morag Smith

Heligan

This dark place
is mud-bound
Underground
Sub-stratum
of a sub-culture
Found in rough bark
memories of goats
        stiff white hair
        spiking my small hands
        its wild pale eye
        arranged around a small black window
        from which it watches
Found in damp smell
        leaves breaking down into mud
        houses membraned in mould
Found in the dark
        a canopy filtering light
        night walk
        obscurus
        feet finding the edge of the path
Found in the squeak
        of a wheelbarrow
        cutting through mud
        one wheel caking as it cuts

Rabbits

Her trailer leans
old tins on the floor
windows sift dirt from the wind
obscuring the light
'me and you'
she says
'we're queens of the road'
wonders why
she had to teach my son to skin a rabbit

I walk on the dunes
with my German friend
her black hair lifts up
white skin
dotted with red
either side of her tiny nose

Earlier
at home
short legs kicking back
against a damp bale of hay
watching me cook
Betty tells me
as she lights the end of a stick
that she wants to eat a rabbit
She's four years old
gazing into the distance
imagining how it will taste

The wind blows sand
into a soft scoop of dune
filled with a roll of thorns
a pocket
carved by the breeze
a death cry
briefly drowning out the sound
of waves breaking
on a beach we can't see

My friend's proud dog
drags a rabbit from the brambles
lays it at my daughter's feet
takes just the eyes
The child watches as I
grasp its strong back legs
the tendons
like guitar strings
under its silky coat

We walk home
As it swings
the body cools
They watch me
chop its feet and peel its skin
translucent
blue white glow
inside a soft brown furry glove
the dog can have its head
Betty hefts the little axe
but misses
cuts its ear in two
a neat triangle
clean   flat
and strange

Salt of the Earth

Don't call me salt
call me soil
call me dirt
call me unrefined

Behind me
the hill rises up
but under me
the ground is broken

Grubbed in the dark
holder of seeds
turn shit black
I am the fifty foot woman
up to my neck in it

when I merge
into the ground like this
I appear smaller
but be wary
of the depths I sink to

Aiming my eyes at the earth
I look into the dirt
see the disturbances
beneath the surface

The past pulses
through my boots
making the buckles rattle
The Bal maiden
her history
the sorting and sieving
freezes the blood
in my veins
winds up lodged
under my fingernails

Great Flat Lode

All around
uncapped shafts
create slight depressions
in the ground

Spoil
rising gently to the lip
once heaped up
now falls stone by stone
into the dark beneath
chased by echoes
down long walls
of rough rock

Once a man stood here
vanning the land under the hill
standing on rich soil
building a counting house in his mind

Now the surface is
slag
waste from ore
hauled to the light
broken up by men
then spalled
by freezing girls

Infinity Pool

The infinity pool has no edges
as it laps the horizon

Learn to touch
with the in and the out breath

A construction industry
involuntarily abandoned

fragments of capitalism
broken scaffolding

We swim inappropriately
in this borderless pool

our fingers reaching
for the sky

swimming harder
trying to touch that impossible line

Night with a Pocketful of Stones

30/11/2021

Traian T. Coșovei

Translated from the Romanian by:
Adam J. Sorkin & Andreea Iulia Scridon

Electric Snow

I pass through a blue, indecisive snowfall
        as if through a corridor where mechanical birds
    cry on my shoulders with electric tears.

I pass by and the birds carry me at their neck
            suspended between two events,
                with my heart beating between two echoes
        (and collapsed between two bodies, just like a cry
between two mouths hungering for me, waiting for me,
                suddenly wanting me).

I know, I know that it's all very late,
    everything struggles between two electrostatic discs,
but what do you tell me?
            You show me a composition of toothed wheels
    and levers and tell me:
                        Look, these are your parents;
Look, this is your heart – take it and carry it further
        over the shards of this semblance?...
You show me rain digging into the bronze horse and tell me:
    Look, this is the order of things – first you, then you,
then you, and you and you and you and you...

    I pass and the fixed stars above me
    sustain the air between two equal wingbeats
left on my shoulders by the transparent birds of sleep
        (between two echoes, between two equal wingbeats
    I see electric seconds spark
                    then darken,
expand and await and suddenly want me),
    as I, before the magnesium lightning,
start to scream,
            seeming to express something, or just
    falling dead, mouth agape.

[A.J.S./A.I.S.]

Ninsoarea electrică

Trec printr-o ninsoare albastră, nehotărâtă
        ca printr-un coridor unde păsări mecanice
plâng pe umerii mei cu lacrimi electrice.

Trec şi păsările mă poartă la gâtul lor
        suspendat între două întâmplări,
                cu inima bătând între două ecouri
        (şi prăbuşit între două trupuri, aidoma unui strigăt
între două guri înfometate de mine şi aşteptându-mă
                şi dorindu-mă dintr-odată).

Ştiu, ştiu că totul e foarte târziu,
        că totul se zbate între două discuri electrostatice,
dar ce-mi spuneţi voi?
                Îmi arătaţi o alcătuire de roţi dinţate
        şi pârghii şi-mi spuneţi:
                        Iată, aceştia sunt părinţii tăi;
Iată, aceasta este inima ta – ia-o şi poart-o mai departe
        peste cioburile acestei aparenţe...
Îmi arătaţi ploaia săpând în calul de bronz şi-mi spuneţi:
        Iată, aceasta este ordinea – întâi tu, apoi tu,
apoi tu, şi tu şi tu şi tu şi tu...

    Trec şi deasupra mea stelele fixe
susţin aerul între două bătăi de aripi egale
lăsate pe umerii mei de păsările transparente ale somnului,
        (între două ecouri, între două bătăi de aripi egale
        văd secundele electrice strălucind,
                        apoi înnegrindu-se,
        umflându-se şi aşteptându-mă şi dorindu-mă dintr-odată),
                în timp ce eu, în faţa fulgerelor de magneziu
încerc să strig,
                părând că exprim ceva, sau numai
        căzând mort cu gura deschisă.

The Land Behind the House

to my father

"The land behind the house will go
to your older brother," said the father as distance
fell over those who were looking at him with no understanding.
    (Until they came to understand anything, the animals of the field
    grazed silently upon the sparkling grass
    that had grown over my father's words.)

"This land you have conquered by blood,"
said the general falling from his horse before his soldiers
who were looking at him with no understanding.
Until they came to understand (one, two, three, four...),
until they came to understand anything,
a twenty-two cannon salute in honour of the general
fell over them like melons rolling down from a roof in the dark of au-
tumn.

After a while just the horse was left.
Years later, the horse would win the Grand Stakes
racing on a famous track.

As for the general, long ago he had divided the land
behind the house
among those who were still looking at his monument
with no understanding, with no understanding.

[A.J.S/M.N.]

304

Pământul din spatele casei

tatălui meu

Pământul din spatele casei să-l dați
fratelui vostru mai mare – spuse tatăl când
depărtarea căzu peste cei care îl priveau fără să înțeleagă.
    (Iar până să înțeleagă ei ceva, animalele câmpului
        smulgeau tăcute o iarbă strălucitoare
        crescută peste cuvintele tatălui.)

Pământul acesta l-ați cucerit cu sânge,
spuse generalul căzând de pe cal în fața soldaților care
îl priveau fără să înțeleagă.
Iar până să înțeleagă ei
(una, două, trei, patru...), până să înțeleagă ei ceva,
douăzeci-și-două de salve de tun în onoarea generalului
căzură peste ei ca pepenii rostogoliți din pod,
toamna, pe întuneric.

După o vreme a rămas doar calul,
care ani mai târziu câștiga marele premiu
alergând pe un mare hipodrom.

Iar generalul își împărțise demult pământul din
spatele
casei celor care îi priveau și acum monumentul
neînțelegând, neînțelegând.

Night with a Pocketful of Stones

It might be that you exist
in this very night, in a bullet fired into the flesh of memory.

With a thousand faces
you might be staring at the mirror where time is a frozen lake
                                    with frozen skaters –
a city lit by the electrified tiles of the cats on its roofs.

And where your life is a pearl,
a pea bundled against nature's breast
among mastiffs, tourists and burning tents, tattered and bloody –
although not even enamelled tin Indians show up here,
only the night with its small hand-mirror, to see who's still breathing,
                        who's still moving, who's a traitor.

Here, memory spins a teaspoon round and round
as if winding the mainspring of a clock that, running at last, rediscovers time.
It's a glory measured in light-seconds: from photographs
                        your bicyclist's past beams like an idiot
(perfumed spokes with which time pedals backwards...)

Maybe this world is nothing but a wire
strung across the frozen darkness of the stars –
a cable through which we're transmitted from somebody's voice
                                    to somebody else's.
A whisper beseeching the fiery ear of a sunbeam...
A scream ripping the membrane of the enormous microphone of night.

It might be that you exist
in a night with a pocketful of stones,
when every wish is a nose flattened against the shop window
(when every word is a mouse waiting for the shock of morning)
and the sky
is a child's design on an asphalt sidewalk
                which the stick of the blind, anyhow, won't ever understand.

[A.J.S./L.V.]

Noapte cu buzunarele pline de pietre

S-ar putea să exişti
în noaptea asta, într-un glonte tras în carnea memoriei.

Cu o sută de chipuri
ai putea să priveşti oglinda în care timpul
       e-un lac îngheţat cu patinatori cu tot, –
un oraş luminat de ţiglele electrizate ale pisicilor de pe acoperişuri.

Şi unde viaţa ta e o mărgică,
e o mărgică de mazăre legănată la sânul naturii
printre dulăi, vilegiaturişti şi corturi aprinse, smulse şi însângerate –
deşi, până aici, nu ajung nici măcar indienii de tablă vopsită
ci numai noaptea cu-o oglinjoară, să vadă cine mai suflă,
                       cine mai mişcă, cine trădează.

De-aici, memoria răsuceşte linguriţa de ceai
ca pe arcul unui ceas ce, alergând, redescoperă timpul.
E o glorie măsurată în secunde-lumină: din fotografii
           zâmbeşte ca un idiot trecutul tău de ciclist
(spiţe parfumate pe care timpul pedalează înapoi...)

Poate că lumea asta nu e decât o sârmă
traversată de întunericul îngheţat al stelelor, –
un cablu prin care trecem din glasul cuiva

                   spre altcineva.
O şoaptă implorând la urechea fierbinte a razei...
Un strigăt strivind membrana uriaşului microfon al nopţii.

S-ar putea să exişti
într-o noapte cu buzunarele pline de pietre,
când fiecare dorinţă e un nas turtit de-o vitrină
(când orice cuvânt e un şoarece aşteptând şocul dimineţii)
şi cerul
e un desen de copil, pe asfalt,
       pe care bastonul orbului oricum nu-l poate pricepe.

There Are Angels Walking the Fields

30/11/2021

Marlon Hacla

Translated from the Filipino by:
Kristine Ong Muslim

Invocation

In the name of the rock. In the name of the lily blossom.
In the name of white paint smeared across a tomb.
In the name of the skull. In the name of marble statues
Of dwarves in the garden. In the name of the pocketknife
Thrust into a pipit's heart. In the name of burned
Letters from a concubine. In the name of letters
Making up your name. In the name of your nocturnal name.
In the name of the moon. In the name of the sun.
In the name of the eclipse. In the name of the eyes
Of a blind child. In the name of pigs
Killed for the fiesta. In the name of chicks
Dyed for the fiesta. In the name of children
Who had nothing to eat. In the name of children who had no one to play with
But themselves. In the name of wives
Abandoned by their husbands. In the name of gay fathers.
In the name of forgotten poems. In the name of people
Who did not have their pictures taken. In the name of lips
Never kissed. In the name of hands
Never held. In the name of faces hidden
By a black veil. In the name of ears
That had not known the sound of a violin. In the name of a flower
That bloomed in the morning and wilted by nightfall.
In your name, you who would someday die and fade away.

Imbokasyon

Sa ngalan ng bato. Sa ngalan ng liryo.
Sa ngalan ng puting pinturang ipinahid sa puntod.
Sa ngalan ng bungo. Sa ngalan ng marmol na estatuwa
Ng mga duwende sa hardin. Sa ngalan ng lansetang
Itinarak sa puso ng pipit. Sa ngalan ng mga sinunog
Na liham ng kalaguyo. Sa ngalan ng mga titik
Ng iyong pangalan. Sa ngalan ng iyong pangalan
Sa gabi. Sa ngalan ng buwan. Sa ngalan ng araw.
Sa ngalan ng eklipse. Sa ngalan ng mga mata
Ng bulag na paslit. Sa ngalan ng mga baboy
Na pinatay para sa pista. Sa ngalan ng mga sisiw
Na kinulayan para sa pista. Sa ngalan ng mga batang
Walang makain. Sa ngalan ng mga batang walang ibang makalaro
Kundi ang kanilang mga sarili. Sa ngalan ng mga inang
Iniwan ng kanilang asawa. Sa ngalan ng mga baklang ama.
Sa ngalan ng mga nalimot na tula. Sa ngalan ng mga taong
Hindi nakunan ng larawan. Sa ngalan ng mga labing
Hindi nahalikan. Sa ngalan ng mga kamay
Na hindi nahipo. Sa ngalan ng mga mukhang itinatago
Sa itim na tela. Sa ngalan ng mga taingang
Hindi nakarinig ng tunog ng biyolin. Sa ngalan ng bulaklak
Na bumuka sa umaga at nalanta sa takipsilim.
Sa ngalan mo na isang araw, papanaw at lilipas din.

The Starry Night, Vincent Van Gogh

Suppressed moans can still be heard
Next door.
Someone watches, whimpers
Through a window not too far from here.
My love, blue is what mantles
The night stretched over all rooftops.
Demons convene
On the leaves of black undergrowth.
They are preparing to invade
Us in our sleep.
It is possible they've managed to entomb
Our sanity.
Rest your head
Against my shoulder, my love.
Let us watch the rolling
Of the skies.

De sterrennacht, Vincent van Gogh

Pumupuslit ang mga ungol
Sa kabilang bahay.
May dumudungaw, tumatangis
Sa isang bintana, di kalayuan.
Mahal, bughaw ang kumot
Ng gabi sa lahat ng bubungan.
Nagtipon ang mga demonyo
Sa mga dahon ng itim na halaman.
Naghahanda sa pagsakop
Sa ating pag-idlip.
Marahil sa burol nila itinatago
Ang ating katinuan.
Ihilig ang iyong ulo
Sa balikat ko, mahal.
Panoorin natin ang paggulong
Ng kalawakan.

The Playground

The first child arrived and noticed the bare
Surroundings. When he realized he was alone,
He created an invisible friend to play with.
The second child arrived and was taught
By the first child how to make
An invisible playmate.
The only thing missing, then, was a game.
They thought of asking for money but remembered
They had no parents.
Hence, they constructed a playground
No one else could see: here was the wooden horse,
Over there were the trees, with a hammock, and there,
They could swing over the cavorting birds.
They spent all day building all sorts of things and structures.
The next day, they established an entire city.
The second child's restlessness caused him to trip and fall down,
Smash his mouth against the ground, lose two of his teeth.
They made a tight lattice with their adjoined palms, imagined
They were connecting bits and pieces of mirrors.
They exchanged faces.
They put together a guardian angel
So they wouldn't ever again know hurt.
In time, the children lost interest and tore down their city.
They thought playing ball sounded more fun.
And so they created balls.
Four balls.
They played hide-and-seek among the trees
That were invisible. Met each other's gaze.
Daily they played catch.
There were moments of happiness
But they were restless their whole lives..

Ang Palaruan

Dumating ang unang bata at napansing hubad
Ang paligid. Nang matantong nag-iisa siya,
Gumawa siya ng kalarong hindi nakikita.
Dumating ang ikalawang bata at tinuruan siya
Ng unang bata kung paano gumawa
Ng kalarong hindi nakikita.
Ang tanging problema'y wala silang lalaruin.
Naisip nilang humingi ng pera pero naalala
Nilang wala na silang mga magulang.
Kaya gumawa sila ng palaruang
Hindi nakikita: dito ang kahoy na kabayo,
Doon ang mga puno, diyan ang duyan, at doon,
Sa ibabaw ng mga naglalandiang ibon sila maglalambitin.
Maghapon silang gumawa ng mga bagay at estruktura.
Kinabukasan, nakabuo sila ng siyudad.
Dahil sa kalikutan, nadapa ang ikalawang bata,
Sumubsob ang bibig, at natanggalan ng dalawang ngipin.
Pinagdikit-dikit ng mga bata ang mga palad at inisip
Na iyo'y pinagdugtong-dugtong na salamin.
Nagpalit sila ng mga mukha.
Gumawa sila ng bantay na anghel
Upang hindi na sila masaktan kailanman.
Paglaon, nagsawa ang mga bata at giniba ang siyudad.
Naisip nilang mas mainam na laruan ang bola.
Kaya gumawa sila ng mga bola.
Apat na bola.
Nagsipagtago sila sa mga punong
Hindi nakikita. Naghulihan ng mga titig.
Araw-araw silang nagbatuhan.
May panaka-nakang sandali ng saya
Ngunit habambuhay silang naging maligalig.

Dirt

30/11/2021

Dominic Leonard

Dollhouse

There was a mother
who fell back,
assiduously. I'm
most people are
always worrying
it is so difficult;
the world or
the world is
not enough. No
one really is alive
more than I am
alive, secured
to the sot & thrall
of the hurling thing,
aloft on the bough
of me; the boy I'd
want to know
is a fraud, hurting
blue, as a star retains
its hidden crush –
his swallow
of dark, his frame of
burning, a lit hilltop fir –
o glory to the
ground where I can
make a locket of this
body, to keep it,
to be not here only.

What is the wind, what is it

after Gertrude Stein

An egg – lithe beast that could crack with any pressure,
That gets yellower towards its centre, that hangs between
The fingers. A ghost-vision, serenely bovine. Incubated,
Stratified. A correct language of where it was, where it
Went, how are we anchored by it. But, to wander with it –
How the wind knocks my ham-fisted breath from me,
Makes a pelt of it. And wedged is the wind, trickling
Into and out of all my little compartments and rooms,
A fawn in a field seen blurred through the rain at nearly
Seven in the evening after stumbling from the house.
Something to consider when deciding on materials to
Rebuild the world from after testing its capacity for grief,
Which is all this was.

Death Poem

I dreamed I was on a pier with Ingmar Bergman,
We must have been in one of the early films
As everything was black and white.

He was irritable because I was
Bothering him with questions and he was doing something
With rope and tools.

What are your films about?
I asked. He sighed
And put the tools down. TIME, he said,

And pay attention to the water.
But I don't remember any water in *Wild Strawberries* (1957), I said,
And only the beach scene in *The Seventh Seal* (1957).

Then you weren't watching closely, he said, and besides,
I've more films than that. He went back to his work.
Later, as he tied those great black knots, he said:

Watch the way the water behaves. You'll see
What they are about; seeing each other,
How you see through things, reflection. Ah!

I said, so they are about more
Than just TIME! Well, he said, looking out at the sea,
Perhaps you have got me there.

Iafnlengd

Where have you been, where are you, stay
    Indoors tonight. You can't tell behind your
Herb-stuffed sleepmask but the design

    Of the streets & gardens has gone awry. *Rock-
A-bye-baby*— you sleep well but yr sheep howl
    & suffer in the lightning-scaffolded fields.

Cast off, no-one is too lonely at sea. *In the tree
    Top*— to sleep is to give up, *when the wind blows* back
To sleep: infinitive. Exclamation. Command.

    As clockwork, *the cradle will rock* & you
Are putting yr fist through glass to sleep, to sleep,
    You are scarred with yr starting. Come, come,

You're lifeless like porcelain & sudden as toothache.
    When the bough breaks the cradle
Delirious breathless potent *will fall*. Fingers

    As cotton & eggshell, branches as unanchored
& serious beings. *& down will come baby.*
    I do you wrong to take you out o the bed— you,

Unguarded somnambulant among the brass & fineries
    Tentatively lifting & dropping yr name
Like feathers, like a confession, *cradle & all*—

O

dear moon i have forgotten your name again , forgive me .
o ragged dreamcatcher moon , o empty theatre moon .   it is cold
down here i cant feel my fingers .   dear moon i am drunk on light
and thinking about how churches look after dark .   do you
ever feel distracted by the sunset ?   it is very cold .   o
toothache moon o chessboard moon , drive me home .   dear moon
down here it is exciting to go to bed with your shoes on
and sometimes i wonder if im only biting my tongue to stop you
from hearing my teeth chattering .   moon i have never sold my body
for less than it was worth .   down here it is easy to forget
about ecstasy .   o wet underbelly of moon covered in twigs
from sleeping in the hedges , you are a heaven waiting to be poured
out .   i have written this in condensation , i hope thats ok .   you
were never one for mementos .   down here everything is fine .
o silver foil moon .   o vulnerable , triumphant moon .
o locked bathroom cabinet of moon it is ok to make mistakes .
i hate to see you sat huddled under the window like that ,
wont you come back to bed .   im sorry to say most nights
i can hear you talking to yourself , dont worry .   dear moon
i am scared about everything too .   o old cabbage moon
from down here you look as smooth as an oboe but i know
you have secrets .   i know the rooms within a scar .   o dearest
moon , i love the nights like these .   the sky gets so complicated .
its nights like these that make me wish i could do your cold job
for you .   keeping the sky upright , washing the heavy hills.

Monomaniac

30/11/2021

Liam Bates

Monolith

I notice it one morning, all
fifty feet, projecting from a square
of lawn at the far end of the garden.
Dad insists it's always been there:
he's sure we brought it with us
from the house where we used to live,
but I find this difficult to stomach,
me not seeing earlier, given its shadow
falls right across my window
for most of the day, its glassy grey
surface throwing light back, dazzling
prying neighbours and low-flying birds.
I would have noticed. Except growing
flush round its base is a daffodil rim
in uninterrupted spring bloom, which fits
with what Dad says or at least implies
the monolith didn't land or spring up
overnight. There's no chance these flowers
could survive that unscathed. I watch them,
a row of dancing stars like a halo
concussion round a cartoon's head.

Monosyllabic

In here, glass is like cash. A shard
from a vase or jar is good to trade.
I sneak a piece of fish bowl in my shoe
heel. When the head nurse asks me
for the truth I say, No, I'm clean,
and think of my pet fish in his cup.
Most kids find a crack in the wall
or a grate they can lift to hide
their stash. Mine is in a hole
at the foot of my quilt. I think
the plan is to hoard till there's
glass to make a full pane out of,
to look through it and catch
sight of the sun in the sky. This
one girl, a teen like me, she's been
in here for a long time. She's stored
so much glass she can build a whole
door to slide back, step through
and walk off site. A bell rings,
a light flares in the hall. When
it's been three hours at least and they
in some way get her back, she screams
so loud a nurse has to pin her to the floor,
with a jab to the side to help her sleep.
I watch this all from the lounge. I sit
in a worn blue chair and sip my warm
not too hot cup of tea. I should move.
If I'm quick, I can find out where
they take her glass while she's out cold.
    Monophagous

I've settled on the medium
of glass for my magnum opus,
but there's no time to learn how
to blow hot glass into shape.
You have to understand, art,

it's not about getting really good at stuff.
I've used empty wine bottles—lashed
them together with bandages.

It's said we have at least one
novelty in us: I've tried to tap
into that secretive vein.
It's said too you never forget your first
blackout. The floorboards are cool
and true on my face. Whole hours

or days have vanished and hanging
over me, this sculpture. I guess
I must've transcended. It's huge,
almost life-sized and just
as ugly as I intended.

Monosemic

Lately I keep regaining consciousness
in a dimly lit corridor with a torch in my face.

A nurse asks my name and address, says
to write it on a piece of paper. I do

as she asks., but it's wrong. I've ruined
the spelling. I've drawn a grey symbol. It's

vaguely phallic. The nurse shakes her head
and asks me to wait as she checks on the system

to find out where I'm meant to be and
why I'm so far from there. While she's busy

in another room, I try to remember how
to operate my body. I gain some control

of my lower half—enough to escape through
a fire exit. As I push down on the bar,

an alarm starts blaring. I step into the daylight
of an unfamiliar cityscape. The pavement

and my joggers are caked with vomit.
A taxi driver shakes his head
at the question of me going anywhere.

Monosaccharide

If I had a job by now, I'd have saved myself
enough money to quit my job and take

a bus to the airport and a plane out to
anywhere. I could sit in a window seat,

watch the grey squares of the city shrink away.
I could drink a white wine out of see-through

plastic. I could sleep through
what's left of the journey. I've heard across the sea

they have mountains with gods at their peaks.
I could pack my hiking boots and head up there.

I'd sleep dreamless and not gnash my teeth.
I'd buy a better toothbrush and start flossing.

I've typed up a list of aspirations in all
caps and tacked the printouts to the wall

above my bed. They exist as concrete
objects now—they won't disappear

when the future's fickle aperture
shrinks to a pinhole.

Monorail

I once got so scared of dawn's sober approach,
resorted to wandering streets for a night that lasted
a year, home somehow the far side
of the train depot, but I'd turned into

this estate and gotten all spun around. In the
airglow, all those grey structures looked
fifty feet tall and identical. Looking back

on that time, I picture a maze misprinted
on the back of a pub kitchen's kids menu:
a tantrum swirl of grey crayon. There's this

question posed by historians of how
best to memorialise a tragic event.
In most of the circles that ask it's accepted
the purpose is not just to build a museum

to be walked around leisurely, holding up
colourful maps and walkie-talkie audio guides.
It should be remembrance of what's lost, yes—

but also an uncomfortable reminder
of what doesn't bear repeating. It should hurt
to occupy that space again. So why

is there a drawer in my wardrobe, chock full
of hideous commemorative t-shirts? My
kitchen cupboards are stacked with souvenir
glassware I'd never want a guest to find.

Aurora Town

31/12/2021

Annie Katchinska

Music of another church

Alleluia – a story of want –
Alleluia, in root beer tongues
He is a good warrior in his tight jacket
Alleluia, felt tip, Alleluia, God-wristband
Aquarium lights say to me, Alleluia
Anthems say, Alleluia
And snow like heaps of polar bears in all directions, Alleluia
Alleluia, wherever you are – you're with the BBC
Consequently no longer foreigners, strangers
Alleluia, cute friend, let us pray for your headache
Alleluia lay our hands Alleluia Alleluia
She's an angel with a microphone, Alleluia
My heart to be scrubbed, Alleluia
Alleluia, fall on your knees
Alleluia, blister of a Sunday
Altar call –
Tick off your sins –
And this girl with no gift but you, Alleluia, no skin
Until I touched you, no words until I spoke you,
I offer my tortoiseshell eyes for you to peel off,
I didn't know water until I was up
And it splashed around me like nothing, a promise
To never go back
Alleluia, never
Forget – but now –
Our bodies stumpy sticks of chalk
Flamingo Motel, Alleluia
Intentional, Alleluia
Our guilty worshipful Alleluia
Our worshipful skins
And a long bright list of what you are not
And my body crumbly with shame, Alleluia
Apocrypha, Alleluia
Again they would say Rejoice Rejoice
No shortage of butter here in milk heaven
Don't wrestle from the bunch, little grapes
But Alleluia, wrestle – twist –
Alleluia, Dead Sea
Alleluia, taste it
O taste and gargle and spit

Negative Pocket

HERE WE GO the woman says opening the door to the insect circus

this is where beetles tremble in ice

wind up the tightropes

sorry for disturbing

all weekend I don't actually speak

I stack tin cans in an earthquake kit

a bluebottle towers by the trapdoor

five hundred yen for the beak of a crow

the boy who was screamed at this morning

drinks carton after carton of milk

until his classmates forgive him

kanji fall down the chalkboard like snow

in a corner marked CROWS there's a glow worm in a box

hot eggy cabbagey pancake

potato curry baguette

glittery fleas stuck round a mirror where you can see my shins

a dirty flying ant

battling my breath's

clumsy cartwheels

it comes down

the snow comes very sorry

I stagger to the trapdoor's delicate sign

PLEASE TOUCH THE BLUEBOTTLE GENTLY

Wherever the body is

My soul doth magnify the Lord
who melts the snow in grubby, chunky heaps.
As stretches of honest pavement reappear it gets safer

to shed jumpers, take deeper breaths,
wake up at sunrise and fold the futon,
and go to church. I want to run –

I want to run to run to what,
for what? Is this a phase –
For he hath regarded the lowliness of his handmaiden

who folds a page of her new NIV
in the karaoke room, mid-afternoon,
and clicks open her pen.

The reason the world does not know us –
it did not know him. What would I ask him?
In the spangly tenth-floor cabin I scribble,

A handful of beautiful, freshly cut jewels,
Continually cleansed until we get to heaven,
I don't want, I can't let this be just a phase.

Wherever the body is
(new patches of grass, corn stalls, businessmen
hack into cobs

as we open the doors, set up the chairs,
position the lights) there the eagles
will be gathered together.

Friday night – pizza party.
Hi I'm from London, yes London, a meaningless sound.
Create in me a clean heart, O my rope.

Aurora Town

Listen   Listen   Listen to me   Let me tell you
what I've learned so far   Among sesame powders,
scallops on sticks a single cut of horse sashimi
is red and costly like a small tongue   A woman
sits across from me and says by thirteen she was
speaking in tongues   She tells me it feels like
bubbling water   She asks would I like to come
with them past bubbling stews   Gaijin bars
RAMEN-CHOCO   Boiled meats on a stick   In your
grid-town we know something good will happen
If we knock   If we listen   Each street a photo,
a bounce to our gestures   The covered walkway
theme tune on a loop   *Sap Po Ro*   In primary
colours   Shivery host boys   High school girls with
graduation flowers   Hitched-up skirts   And how
can they believe if they have not heard and how
can they hear without someone preaching and
how can anyone preach unless they are sent
so I head to the underground shopping streets
or into Starbucks   Tully's   Doutor   La Pausa
McDonald's   Vie de France   Outside the shrine
the dolphin balloons rustle together   Her flip
phone weighed down by toys   I let down the nets
for a catch   Listen   I am the clay, you are the potter
I've learned to feel so strongly for you and to say it
My brain echoes constantly   Thank you thank you
C'mon   C'mon   Can you hear it   She's looking
interested and I say with my newly sweetened
smile   See you Sunday   It feels so good   This
Food Brings Us A Wonderful Time   Matcha
drinks in trembling shades of green with green
ice cream and the girls eat foot-high green
parfaits with dinky spoons   And you tell me
when the storm has swept by the wicked are
gone and I believe you   Junior high school
baseball teams break and shift the old snow
with shovels   The righteous stand firm forever
The spring sun finally bursts, a piñata   Crucible
for silver and furnace for gold   Everything is

personal   Frisbee by the TV Tower   Jingles
Percussion   Vitamin Lemon   NIPPON-HAM
FIGHTERS   Butter Roll   I'm flammable, I'm
getting it right   I know that this is what
you want   Polaroids   Fountains   Revelations
Shaved ice   Can you hear me   Can you

Dream after baptism

Terracotta bath into which I step.
What colour is the room – dim yellow.
The room is very hot (candlelit?). Oval
of water swirling with sparks
off the rim to be electric around me,
prepare me –
Tight red loop of muscle stretched out
holding the dream together.
Wouldn't she like to get married?
What does this mean to her?
To know your morning sun – Bathtub
cold as a pond in hungry greens –
spinning silvers – streaks of
conviction red
with a chime This is possible, possible
shining ever brighter till the full light of day
The path of the righteous.
And then in the name of,
Hold me right down for a long time
longer than the first time, bubbles stream
from me, I dig my nails
into the fish and claw them open.
I crackle all the way through.
No breath now, only a purging.

Waterbearer

31/12/2021

Stuart McPherson

My Daughters Photograph

Europa, I am obsessed   with storms
And you, with orbits
around my waist

          Your face born bright
             and me, unable to bear
               the weight of feet

So beautifully soft blue
   My gravity hasn't failed you yet
               young moon

But maybe the size of space, my
   absorption, my propensity for vastness
        The way that I live out here

Did you see me, Europa?
   Through a telescope or the touch of gravity
          pushing in our lives?

Born free
And here I am, hoping for revival
        That fear won't pull you in

That in absence you might forgive
This process of creation
This mad old way   I seem to spin

Portrait of a Mother

A boy left in the glow
She lay with a man
Door open, covered
with a sheet

They bathed together
He played downstairs
The television was
cruel to him

"Get me a knife" she
said
Such sharp intention
He sharpened himself

Her willowed arms
Blushed cheeks
Reddened teeth
It left from his mouth

He called downstairs
to damp skin
and cramped
like a rose

A room without air
Without eyes
On hands and knees
She coloured him in

All that flesh
Lingerie, breasts
Pursed lips
Hers to own and his

Her swollen eye
Crab shelled
A soaking bed
The purple of night

Everyone knew it
The door knew it
No feet on the mat
No knuckles to knock

She hasn't been seen
for years
An absent magicians
invisible cloak

Every Morning There Are Two of Me

I climb into bed, this long flat knife
The way a surgeon re-opens a slow wound

There are twice the loosening lights
Alpha Aquarii netted in the orange of a bowing lamp

Outside we are ready to be thrown into the long trees
As the street holds the hollow sound of rope

The morning questions a casket lottery

The lies of our rested shapes shepherd away paleness,
like a crook

Self-Help Manual Written in Invisible Ink

And then   as if revolving around the sun   he started to spin
Language a lie   spun by two separate lives
One before   one after   *He had made it this far*

They kept talking to him about nature   its benefits
He thought about a leaf   blown onto the shelf of a high rock
into seams with all the others never quite seen or   felt
between fingers   and rubbed   into dust

His lungs now thin   and unable to accommodate this
present air   or past   the golden hands of sunlight existing
solely to burn skin   How do you meditate when all you do
is sit lotus legged and see the Ohm as   *just sound released*

These *must- have* strategies   Some preparation for
transcendence   his previous dependence on horoscopes and
zodiacs   His worldly place   in the hands of fate
The chime of Tingsha   no line   no trajectory between what is

or has been   and definitions of identity   all down to
conjunction   Excuses for defunct people
Benign fun / benign body   *What is running but*
the taste of blood on your tongue?   Or a heaving in and out

Some need for self-care   a test   and before she
left   she talked about the way he ignored himself
Something held within   The knowingness of
a peak worn down   beneath water   beneath wind

Something Had to Die So That I Could Live

In the beginning of
beautiful death,
There were no signs

In fading light
pulled out the twins
One white, one still

Motherly clicks
The wetness of hay
Her bleating eyes

Looking, then licked
Swung twice and
slapped

The man wrapping
Aries in a sheet,
took away the old

By the daffodils
set him down
Whilst the new

Danced in the grass
Like snow
for the beautiful dead

sometimes I write poems and sometimes I write poems

31/12/2021

Martín Rangel

Translated from the Spanish by: Lawrence Schimel

decaigo como el año

del árbol soy la hoja que se desprende
y aterriza sobre un punto ciego

decaigo como el año
y de las estaciones soy
                      el desfase
la flor que brota en pleno invierno:
un desierto sobre el que no para de llover

solo en el otoño me encuentro,
en otoño coinciden
las vibraciones del mundo y de mi voz

en otoño
donde la hoja cae
sobre tu hombro adolorido
de sostener mi llanto

en otoño
cae la hoja
sobre tus párpados pesados y oscuros
cansados de sobrevivirme

cae la hoja cae como
decae el día como
decae el año
y yo con ellos
        cobrizo
             lento
                   cubierto de un aroma a sal
                         y muerte

i decay like the year

from the tree i'm the leaf that comes loose
and lands on a blindspot

i decay like the year
and of the seasons i am
                        the out of step
the flower that blooms in full winter:
a desert upon which it doesn't stop raining

only in autumn do i find myself,
in autumn they harmonize
the vibrations of the world and of my voice

in autumn
when the leaf falls
upon your shoulder which aches
from upholding my grief

in autumn
the leaf falls
upon your heavy, dark eyelids
tired of surviving me

the leaf falls it falls like
the day decays like
the year decays
and i with them
        copperish
                slowly
                        covered by the scent of salt
                        and death

BIG DATA

todo es pasajero y
todos somos pasajeros
           del mismo
vehículo suicida

nunca confíes en los instintos

           baja por favor
los codos de la mesa

levanta el rostro

           y sonríe

no olvides que estás siendo filmado

BIG DATA

everything passes and
we are all passengers
        of the same
suicidal vehicle

never trust your instincts

        please take
your elbows off the table

lift your chin

        and smile

don't forget that you're being recorded

"el tiempo pasa más lento cuando no puedes dormir" confirmó la ciencia

y nunca terminamos de mirar al sol marcharse
y nunca estuvimos muriendo todo se trataba de un performance
cerramos los ojos y pudimos ver flores pero no pudimos olerlas
recuerdo un rastro interminable de sudor y glitter
y música que sonaba muy fuerte   ser solamente
cuerpo   recuerdo que atravesé el espejo y no había nada
del otro lado de las cosas   no te pierdes de mucho
cosas comunes como el insomnio o los eclipses
o fracturas en el pecho o diagnósticos médicos poco alentadores
o el miedo al insomnio
                        (que a veces es peor)
de todas las cosas que he ido olvidando con el tiempo
cómo vivir es la que más echo de menos
pero seguro que alguien ya subió
un tutorial en youtube al respecto
que difícilmente me enseñará a vivir
pero seguro me entretendrá el insomnio

"time passes slower when you can't sleep" science confirmed

and we never finish watching the sun go down
and we were never all dying it was a performance
we close our eyes and could see flowers but not smell them
i remember an interminable face of sweat and flitter
and music playing strongly   to be just
body   i remember i crossed through the mirror and there was nothing
on the other side of things   don't miss many
common things like insomnia or eclipses
or fractures of the chest or not encouraging medical diagnoses
or the fear of insomnia
                              (which sometimes is worse)
of all the things i've forgotten over time
how to live is the one i most miss
but i am sure that someone has already posted
a tutorial on youtube about this
which will hardly show me how to live
but will sure amuse my insomnia

PROSE

Stravaig:
A Fiction for Voices

31/01/2021

David Wheatley

Dramatis personae

AISLING, young woman.
HECTOR, rural gent.
ARTHUR, middle-aged man.
MRS MCGILLIVRAY, religious enthusiast.
EILIDH, jogger.
PERCY, toddler.
SADHBH, child in arms.
BOY, passer-by.

SCENE: rural Aberdeenshire.

[*Sound of pram wheels and the opening bars, piano part only, of Schubert's 'Der Leiermann', giving way to distant wind chimes.*]

AISLING: The chimes, the chimes, baby Sadhbh! I hear their tinny music from over the lochans, tossed this way and that on the breeze. If you stand and listen you might fancy they were playing your song. [*Sings.*] 'Up a bogey lane, to buy a penny whistle, a bogey man came up to me…' Foolish fancy. But when all you hear, all day, is your mother's voice, perhaps all voices melt into my voice, all melt into one. [*Baby gurgles.*] For you, I mean. [*Baby gurgles.*] And for me too, the sound of my voice tossed and returned to me on the breeze. [*Pause.*] Now, is it this or the next turn. Dalmadilly, land of the… whortleberry. Whortleberries, to put on your porridge, baby Sadhbh! But where is that father of yours, off at his Pictish stones again. An 'incomparable recumbent', he said, just past the woods. Perhaps he is taking a rubbing of the inscription. Lovely day for it though, to disappear down a back lane between the high hedges. And what sharp heat, as sharp as the spikes on the gorse. But will he have remembered to water the boy… the *bairn*, though, I wonder. And will the youngster have a clean bottom? Imagine how an unchanged load in his nappy would chafe the poor thing, baby Sadhbh, and your Daddy so forgetful, with his mind on his bits of old rock. Granite, gabbro or norite: just saying the names is ever so cosy, and the touch of my boy's fingers trailed along the moss in search of a ladybird or a beetle… But is that a ladybird on your hand, baby Sadhbh? Let me count the spots… [*Sound of a passing van.*] What's that curse o' God… [*Mumbles.*] Well bless us and save us, it's farmer Finlay's lorry on its way to market this fine morning! Can you see the poor sheep reaching their snouts out the side? Is it for shearing they're being taken, or… the other thing? It was just the other month the lambs were slipping on their placentas wherever you looked, and look at them now! The grown sheep I mean, unless it's their mothers he's transporting, or both. [*Pause.*] Merrily off to slaughter. [*Pause.*] Of course they feel nothing, they'd have you believe. [*Emphatic.*] There'll be no meat eaten in the house and you growing up, baby Sadhbh! But what have I done to save the wee beasties, their poor tongues hanging from their drouthy mouths? And farmer Finlay reached a hand out the window, too, as he passed, in salutation. [*Vehement.*] I should rebuff him angrily, the puce-faced old brute. He shoots crows too, you know, I've seen them hanging from his fence. [*Baby gurgles. Calmer.*] What terrors await our heedless neighbours, baby Sadhbh when our mask of civility slips. [*Cackles.*] Terrors, I say. [*Pause. A gust of wind.*] But what's that blowing across my face? Why, it's may blossom, stripped from the trees and strewing the road before us. Consider it a good omen. Unlike those malevolent crows – craws – up ahead. I see you! Some birds scurry and others hop, why is that. [*Pause.*] Even collecting carrion, crossing the road to a juicy disaster left in the wake of a passing lorry, they hop. [*Pause.*] Rather than trudge, trudge-push, push. [*Pause.*] The swing from season to season here is savage, baby Sadhbh, simply savage. Tonight I will watch the last of the evening light disappear through the curtains behind Millstone Hill at almost eleven, yet six months ago 'darkness was the universe', as the poet said, and will be again. Just as you were making your appearance. How we hunkered – bunkered – down together through those Arctic nights. My little seed of light, sprouting into our difficult spring and now this unending summer-long daylight! How to reconcile these extremes we hurtle between, hurtle-trudge. I cannot. All I can do is push the wheels round from moment to moment. You are my load and yet it is you who spirit me along, so uncomplainingly too. [*Baby gurgles.*] And on we go to the garden centre, with our menfolk lurking somewhere *en route*. How will young Percy hail us though: yesterday it was [*adopts child's voice*] 'I saw an octagon, Mammy'. Precocious soul. He meant a stop sign. Of course it's all parroting, really, but what am I but a parrot too, turning my jabberings over on my tongue like sweets someone else has sucked first. And yet when I ask him, 'who am I Percy, what's Mammy's name', he will say nothing. Merely stand and stare before running away. [*Mock-serious.*] Poor Percy, with his mind on higher things. [*Pause.*] Who am I, though. Someone must know. I must ask my husband. [*Pause.*] To think it is nearly a decade since we arrived here though, baby Sadhbh! I say we, but you'll pardon the flourish. A decade since I... slipped away from it all, down below. [*Pause.*] Mother. Your voracious ghost. What is it now, a decade I said. [*Pause.*] Sometimes I fancy I am back, or never left. But no. [*Pause.*] All best left dead and buried [*Pause.*] It was a dark December when we arrived. All I had wanted was a mountain to huddle under, and there it was, my granite peak by the river, and I somewhere in the folds of its skirt. As a child I would garble the border ballads, bending my vowels this way and that. [*Sings.*] 'As I was walkin all alane, /I heard twa corbies makin a mane.' [*Baby cries.*] Yes, makin a mane, baby Sadhbh! [*Baby cries.*] There, there, perhaps you fancy a bit of breast, why don't I slip down the banks of rose willow herb and feed you by the river. [*Irritated.*] Bother those clegs! Rose willow herb, also known as fireweed. An invasive species, springing up like that along road-sides, leaving no gap unfilled. [*Sound of pushing through high grass. Surprised exclamation.*] Hector! What are you stalking in that outlandish garb? My word though, your tweeds are incomparable!

HECTOR: Aafa fine the day.

AISLING: I don't dispute it. I knew another Hector once. A bull of that name on the Isle of Eigg, left free on the beach to wander where he wished, 'like some fierce tempest that sweeps down upon the sea'. I had the good fortune to view him from behind as he went on his rounds, his lucky bag bouncing with every step.

HECTOR: The wife says I –

AISLING: Spare my blushes, please –

HECTOR: There's a bull in Morrison's field would run you through for sport.

AISLING: But what *are* you doing footering around here, Hector.

HECTOR: I heard tell of an osprey in these parts, come across from Lochter, and thought it might enliven my morning stravaig. But there won't be much fishing for it here.

AISLING: And is that an eagle I see on your fence-post of an evening?

HECTOR: Buzzard. You'll see a buzzard and mistake it for an eagle, but not see an eagle and mistake it for a buzzard.

AISLING: Ah, my greedy gaze, hungry as a hawk for those

visitations. What languorous circles the osprey turns though! Perhaps it might take a lamb – or a baby? Imagine those claws sinking into your sleepsuit baby Sadhbh, and the folds of your thighs! And then to be carried away above Bennachie, who knows where. I have read of a baby in Norway left outside a church for a moment and snatched by an eagle. I picture her sleeping when found, in the eagle's nest.

HECTOR: I had a dog once who –

AISLING [*Oblivious.*]: The ghillies on the estates find the nests and club the poor creatures to death. Knee deep in grouse as they go. I hear the rifles from the forest behind the house and wonder what they can be shooting at: clay pigeons, real pigeons… boom!, it goes, for hours on end. I was at large in the woods one day and so distracted I walked straight into a shooter. I remember the cracked veins on his cheeks as he wheeled round to face me, burgundy capillaries flushed with bloodlust, and his rifle cocked in my face. I held his gaze for a moment, the baby strapped to my chest, and he was gone, a wood-kerne snarling back into the bushes.

HECTOR: I'm getting a powerful smell of slurry.

AISLING: I can't help you there. Though we live surrounded by stench, I'm used to it now, inured to the manure. I doubt if there are small parcels of the stuff in that backpack of yours, Hector, but there are in mine. Bags of dog poo, now, you often see suspended from branches in their black bags, like small dark fruits doomed never to flower.

HECTOR: Pine marten scat is fair boggin.

AISLING: Smelly?

HECTOR: I've a pair at the end of the garden.

AISLING: What admirable creatures. Only descending from their perches to spray, soil, or hunt. Not for them these little courtesies we waste our time on.

Light Glyphs

28/02/2021

David Spittle

The American poet John Ashbery has accumulated a vast and unique body of work: with over twenty volumes of poetry; several plays; a collaborative novel (*A Nest of Ninnies*, written with James Schuyler); collected prose and art criticism; two collections of French translations (in addition to translating Rimbaud's *Illuminations*, Pierre Reveredy's *Haunted House*, much of Giorgio de Chirico's *Hebdomeros* and Pierre Martory's *The Landscapist*); and, most recently, re-imagining a 'lost film' screenplay for Canadian director Guy Maddin. Widely translated, influential and bedecked with almost every award (including a Pulitzer and, more recently, the National Medal of Arts awarded by Barack Obama in 2011), Ashbery's poetry continues to beguile, enchant and confuse with its amorphous ventriloquism of American life.

In the spring of 2009, the Harvard Film Archive organised 'John Ashbery at the Movies', a series of films curated in celebration of his passion for cinema. This included filmmakers who have acknowledged Ashbery as an influence (Abigail Child, Nathaniel Dorsky, Phil Solomon) and films chosen by Ashbery himself. In addition to the active role of film in his poetry, one of the other (many) reasons that this programme came into being was Ashbery's illuminating prose on cinema. His essays, on Jacques Rivette, the phenomenon of Louis Feuillade's *Fantômas*, Val Lewton's *The Seventh Victim*, and Edgar G Ulmer's *Detour*, are all insightful, clearly wrought and downright infectious in their palpable enthusiasm. This conversational impulse between mediums can be traced back to early collaborations with the filmmaker and photographer Rudy Burckhardt, to the close friendship with Frank O'Hara (who in turn often collaborated with filmmaker Alfred Leslie), the invigorating artistic circles gathering around the Tibor de Nagy gallery in 1950s and 60s New York, and, in Ashbery's formative and frequent cinema trips during his time living in Paris.

In Ashbery's poetry the influence of cinema emerges in the experiential shifts of attention that a reading of his poems can induce, as opposed to simply existing referentially or in blatant ekphrasis. For instance, the syntactic disjunction of *The Tennis Court Oath* (Ashbery's boldly experimental second collection, 1962) has been discussed by critic Daniel Kane as a poetic equivalence of the editing techniques of surrealist film. The productive instability of both 'surrealism' and 'film', as concepts and experiences, generates a mobile ambiguity that Ashbery's poetry has long embraced. Rather than simply referring to film, it is instead in the ability of his poems to enact and inspire experiences that, moving between understanding and its sensation or a moment and its expression, poetry and cinema can both be brought into permeable awareness. The crossing of artistic boundaries and contexts, gleefully tickled or blurred, is also clearly at work in Ashbery's interest in collage – which is where this discussion begins…

DS

Do you feel your engagement with visual collages (having now had four exhibitions to date) has changed at all since the summers spent with Joe Brainard, and even earlier experiments throughout college?

JA

I suppose my engagement with collages has expanded now that I am able to show them at a gallery. I've been working on them quite a bit this summer and hoping there will be another show.

DS

Could you possibly say a bit about the collaged play, The Inn of the Guardian Angel *(collaged from New York Times obituaries and Hollywood fanzines) that you apparently lent to Guy Maddin during his Seances project?*

JA

He and I were fans of each other's work before we ever met and conversed. His recent Seances is beautiful, and of course I love Archangel, My Winnipeg and The Saddest Music in the World, one of my all-time movie favorites. Yes, The Inn of the Guardian Angel is an abandoned project. The title taken from a children's book by the 19th century French (or Russian) children's author Contesse de Ségur. I abandoned it and sent it to Guy telling him he could "strip mine" it for his next movie. I don't think I wrote anything but the "How to Take a Bath" section in his last film. The actor in that film [Louis Negin] who tells an off-color joke (one that I heard in grade school many a year ago) is a sort-of objet trouvé of Guy's, whom he, Guy, has used in a bunch of films.

DS

Let's talk more about film ...

JA

I've always been a fan of movies, and, even more than that, I think the idea of them has somehow informed my work. Do you know my poem 'The Lonedale Operator' in my book A Wave? I realized one day that nobody had ever written a poem on the all-important subject of the first movie they ever saw, so I proceeded to do so. It sort of wobbles away from that subject towards the end as my poems tend to do!

DS

Could you say a bit about 'John Ashbery at the Movies', the pro-gramme of films coordinated by Haden Guest and Scott Macdonald at the Harvard Film Archive?

JA

First off, 'John Ashbery at the Movies' was quite interesting to me, as I had forgotten some of the films and not seen others. The younger filmmakers who were apparently influenced by me were particularly appealing, notably Abigail Child, who is famous but whom I didn't know before then, and I especially liked Phil Solomon's film The Exquisite Hour. Also the Busby Berkeley and Daffy Duck films were just as I remembered them. I was a little disappointed in a French film called Adieu Léonard, which I had seen many years ago in Paris and remembered as a bizarre and delightful comedy. It was just OK. It was made during the Occupation and has some of the creepy brilliance of many of the films of that time. (One I particularly recommend is Called *Douce* by Claude Autant-Lara, a 19th Century romantic tear-jerker that features the famous character actress Marguerite Moréno as an obnoxious old rich lady).

DS

I once read somewhere that you recommended **The Psycho-tronic Encyclopedia of Film** *(Michael Weldon), do you still have this? I have a copy (as a result of that recommendation), it's an absolute treasure-trove of trash...in all the best ways. I love it. Do you have any other books about or on film that have been important to you?*

JA

I hope I do still have a copy of *The Psychotronic Encyclopedia of Film*, though I haven't seen it around lately. I can't think of other books on film that have been important, except for the Hallowell guides and Leonard Maltin's guides for catching films on TV. That book was useful when I wrote a poem, "They Knew What They Wanted," where every line was a movie title that began with "they."

DS

Are there any other poets that share your particular taste in movies? Or poets whose work flirts with film in ways that interest you?

JA

Frank O'Hara and I both were on the same wavelength with regard to movies. Also John Yau has written an essay on going to the movies with me, which I haven't read in a long time, but is quite probably very informative. Robert Polito writes interestingly about film in his poetry.

Two of your favourite films, **On Approval** *(1944) and* **Dead of Night** *(1945), showcase the charms of British actress "Googie" Withers (Georgette Lizette Withers)* ...
JA

By coincidence I saw *On Approval* and *Dead of Night* just a few weeks ago on TV. The marvelous channel Turner Classic Movies had a sort of mini Googie festival, which also included *It Always Rains On Sunday,* which as its title would suggest is rather dreary. I first saw *Dead of Night* sometime in the late forties, at a time when I used to view movies serially. I probably saw it around 20 times along with such other faves as René Clair's *Le Million* and Clive Brook's *On Approval,* maybe my all-time favorite. Bea Lillie was magnificent as the wealthy spinster Maria Wislack and Googie Withers perhaps even greater as the nice person in the movie. It's funny about *Dead of Night.* When I first saw it in Boston in the 40s the golf links sequence wasn't shown, I had to wait until my 16th or 17th viewing in order to see it. Googie again gives her all, especially when she is about to be strangled by her husband and looks in the antique mirror to discover a strange interior and manages to break the mirror just before her husband, whose name momentarily eludes me, almost does her in. I forgot to mention Cocteau's *Orphée,* which was also part of my compulsive cinema-going.

Slaughter

31/03/2021

Rosanna Hildyard

Offcomers

Ravenseat, North Yorkshire.
2001

I wake up because he is not snoring.

I turn my head. Still dark outside, the moon resting on the moor like a fingernail clipping. His head is on the pillow beside me, and I can see the gleam of his eyeballs. When his voice rasps, it is a shock.

What if we get it, he says.

I blink and mumble. We won't, I say. It won't get as far as us, don't worry.

I'm not worried about *us*, he says, and he spits the *us*. I'm thinking about those fucking tourists down in Catterick. Fucking offcomers.

He is talking about the farmer he pays to shelter our sheep in the valley over winter. It is spring now, lambing time and time for our eight hundred pure-bred Swaledale ewes to come back to the uplands, with us. But we've just heard that all movement of animals is banned until the foot-and-mouth is over.

His tone sends a chill down my spine. Farmers don't talk about other farmers in that way. They're not just colleagues; they are allies in the same fight. No matter how much he might scorn or whinge about his neighbours, he does it with a grudging respect.

This sounds different. They best take care of them, he says, and I know that note of warning, and I feel it in the pit of my stomach: bad things lie ahead in the Catterick farmer's future. Then he rolls onto his side, his back rising up before me, and I can no longer see his open eyes.

I close my own eyes and try not to think of the pigs in the Essex abattoir, hanging dead and cold with blisters on their lip-less mouths. The first cases in England. They say it's spreading north. I wonder how it is that I can't just reach out and touch him – *hey, are you awake?* – and yet I am as unable to do that as if I were paralysed, or frozen, or something was holding my arms behind my back and pinning me down.

I open my eyes again. The moon looks like a thin, curved smile.

*

Sky's all pearly outside next morning, when I get up at six. Place my feet carefully as I go down the bare wood of the stairs, so as not to slip and make noise over his radio. The house is more lived-in than it was last year, when I moved in, but it's still what some people – people who don't get us – might call empty. But it's like he says: we don't need flowery things when all we do here is grab a bite of food, and sleep. Well, OK, I took up the carpet with a pair of shears, when I decided I was here for good, and he let me strip the yellowy, smoke-stained wallpaper – but no more.

I am still thinking about how it was as I cross the stone flags of the kitchen and reach the back door. I pull on overalls on, my own breath curling out before me as I fumble boots on. Smells of dogshite.

Outside, there is a streak of hot pink at the horizon. Shepherd's warning, I think, and mind to check the horoscope later, crossing my fingers in the meantime to ward off bad luck. Himself and the dogs are already down by the cattle grid. They are barking, and the quad bike is revving, and he is shouting at the both of them. Come by Floss; Sky, come by. And then a yell back up to me. Come on, then.

He revs the quad bike, not looking back. What am I waiting for? He is going out, onto the moor, when we have the scant hundred older sheep we kept with us, and no lambs.

I pull my hood up and follow him. Onto the moor, where only curlews rise and sing.

When I was training as a florist, back when I lived with my dad, my boss told me about shipments of exotic flowers carrying stowaways. Tarantulas, poisonous red ants, Black Widows, she'd said, walking her dirty fingernails over the counter. They invade the ecosystem and have no predators. I imagined it: unrolling brown paper on your kitchen table, all a-crackle, when out of the stems squirms some fat, boneless, black thing that has scuttled off before you can move a muscle. And, later, you're trousers-down on the bog or sweating over your onions when you feel a cold snip at your ankle... And that's it, for you.

I told him about the spiders in flowers and he snorted. That's how diseases spread! I said. Maybe there are sheep ticks, or flies, or something!

We were sitting on the sofa. He was shovelling in his baked beans and I was screwed up in a corner, toothing the chocolate off the sides of a Blue Riband and trying not to shiver. Fuck that, he said. Be easy enough if it was a matter of catching a couple of spiders.

You what? I said. Have you ever tried to catch a spider?

He didn't even bother to look up from scraping the baked bean tin. They're bloody great big things, he said. This is a virus. It's carried on the wind.

His brow started going all creased as he stared down into the tin. Then he shook his head abruptly, and cleared his throat. Nineteen-sixty-seven, he said. It got blown northwards by the wind. And in nineteen-eighty it got blown onto the Isle of Wight, from France. It's a windborne virus. But it can be carried on cars, clothes, shoes – those bloody hikers, offlanders, they don't belong here. That's why they've locked the Coast to Coast path down so fast, this time.

He stopped, tipped his head back and shook the last dregs of juice from the tin. I watched his Adam's apple bobbing up and one small orange drip trickling down his beard. He put the can down, sighed and rubbed his jaw, apparently without noticing. Windborne? Wasn't that what people thought in, like, medieval times? I thought. He had to be kidding.

I felt suddenly starving for baked beans, put down my gnawed chocolate bar and got up, glancing at the grey hairs in his beard as I did. Windborne? He was obviously desperate. He'd left school years ago; he needed to have an explanation, I thought. He was older than me, after all.

But that was in late March, and as we watched the news each night, I began to feel a creeping suspicion. It was like an invisible giant was stamping north, county by county: Devon, Wales, one quick stride up into Lancashire, coming for us. We watched its footsteps tracking up the country, and my old world – Tesco and schoolfriends having babies, Afghanistan on TV and catching the bus to town – they just bled away.

And when I realized that's what it was – coming for us – I felt relief, deep down in my gut. I've come to realise that's what you feel, when the worst happens: relief. You should have known. You were right, that plague would descend; and on you, of all people. You knew what you always feared would come to be.

The news didn't stop mentioning it. Far from it; they sounded less and less alarmed, the newsreaders' voices deepening into a kind of warm, resigned apology. *And in the North, the Foot and Mouth crisis continues. Blair talks with... In Cumbria alone...* Decontamination zone. Carcasses. Contiguous cull. Bonfire.

Like him, I started arriving breathlessly for the next update every few hours, hanging back in the doorway so I didn't disturb as he leant over the radio. But I couldn't help it. What is Type O? I'd blurt out. Or: isn't that south of us? No, that's not south, he'd say. Didn't you hear him say there was an outbreak in Berwick, as well? Fool, it's not south of us.

He'd roll his eyes, and turn away. His forehead seemed to be growing like a limestone cliff, those ploughed furrows in his forehead deepening. I'd watch as his massive back disappeared outside, and I'd be left alone, with the shadows creeping around me and only the sound of the wind on the grass like laughter in my ears.

*

I am not a real farmer, like him. The first time I saw this place, I was doing a delivery for my dad. I was only eighteen and could barely drive, but my dad dealt in things that fell off the backs of lorries, as he put it, and wasn't much bothered about shoulds and couldn'ts. Drop this load off at Skabbawath, will you? he said, one winter morning as he sat like a fat old woodlouse curled up in his chair. Everyone's bloody fucked me over, again. I don't know why everything's against me. Sod's Law, whatever I try to do...

He whined on about this for a bit, about how the whole world turned just to spite him, bringing up my mum again, then sighed piteously as he wound round to the point ... Least *you* could do is help your dad out, once in a while, all right?

OK, Dad, I said, pushing my hair off my face. Skabba-where?

It was all right, the florists. People never ordered more than the most basic type of bouquet. I spent a lot of time spray-painting chairs gold for my old schoolfriends' weddings. Not much point getting your diploma, eh, pet! my old boss used to cackle. But it was OK. I liked the idea of it, I think. Being there at the most meaningful rituals of people's whole lives, that kind of thing. I'd end up like my boss, I sort of vaguely thought. A bit weird, probably with bad teeth, but at least not having a spray-painted wedding or getting into the same kind of mess my mum and dad had. They thought they could squeeze life like a lemon in their fists, and look where that had gone and got them. Her, running off to Manchester in a desperate game of catch-up with her youth, ending up turning tricks in Canal Street, if my dad were to be believed. And him, chairbound in a ground-floor flat, railing that the politicians were out to get him, and none of it was fair.

My Glorious Sundays

30/04/2021

Aaron Kent

The Glorious
Sundays

A. DON   01

J. CHASE   02

T. SIN   03

EXPOSITION DE MUSEL
ITA 2012   JOURNAL YOURCHURCHES

ISBN 978-1-913642-41-9
9 781913 642419 >

Exposition de Misere is the first The Glorious Sundays album with Onej Tuocs on drums, and it really feels complete. Onej would go on to join the band, but their work on EdM was initially intended to be as a session drummer, though the vibe caught them and they became a permanent member of the TGS, both on tour and in the studio.

That's not to say there wasn't tension in the band or drama, but they were working on a creative wavelength none of them had ever experienced before. James Chase would later call EdM 'the very first time I knew [The Glorious Sundays] were going to make it.'

The vinyl release of EdM came with a bonus cassette of conversations in the studio. These dialogues contained hints of the dynamics at play within the band, little creative successes and arguments. But a few things are clear listening back:

1. Tommy Sixx is considering leaving the band at the start of the sessions.
2. James Chase and Amme are hooking up.
3. Onej Tuocs has huge influence despite being considered a session musician.
4. James Chase is not looking after himself - too much coffee, too much alcohol, not enough sleep.
5. EdM is the reason Tommy stays in the band.

The first time I depersonalised was when I was 12 in DT class, the memory is a blur but I know, looking back, that I felt something was wrong. I didn't depersonalise after that for almost a year, until I was stood on a balcony in Spain, 13 years old, deciding that I would jump to my death.[1]

When Exposition de Misere came out I was depersonalising heavily and often. I was working night shifts at the Asda in St Austell, and going through the motions. It felt like I was behind a screen, watching myself perform menial tasks, disconnected from my physical self.

The world ceased to exist in the solid, lucid form I had known, and while I assumed it was a side effect of a lifetime of insomnia, it became apparent that it was, in fact, something deeper and more troubling.

---

1   There was a tent, like a massive food tent, below. We were on the seventh or eighth floor, and I was planning how to avoid the tent. At twelve. Planning how to kill myself easiest.

I was four minutes into 'Dictionary of Broken Wings' during a midnight drive when I decided to kill myself.

'This is the path adventure brings / this is the reason the blackbird sings / this is a call for ominous things / this is a dictionary of broken wings'

(A Dictionary of Broken Wings by *The Glorious Sundays*)

It's never quite been stated why Tommy Six was consider-
ing leaving TGS, some have surmised that his reluctance to
carry on began when the band refused tobveer towards the
pop sensibilities he was indulging in with his newfound
love of The Beatles. This rift between styles would later
be quashed in one of the extensive band meetings they'd
have, James Chase was more intrigued by the styling of
bands like Bloc Party; those swirling walls of harmonious
noise, whereas Amme Ron had latched onto Young Fathers.

The clash of styles is what makes Exposition de Misere so
good; it's a symbiotic relationship of genres that has been
hammered into a delicate balance. No part sounds too
different to be discordant, but they never find themselves
beating the same drum. It's in the differences that EdM comes
alive, and where TGS produce what is clearly their magnum
opus, their chef-d'œuvre.

There's a moment, about fifteen seconds before the end of
'But Now the Fox' where, if you listen closely, you can hear
a yelp of excitement from somebody in the studio, a sort of
giddy shout of glee. Some critics felt it was intentional, the
band had chosen to record the noise and lay it over the track,
but others saw it as a spontaneous burst of joy in the studio. If
the official TGS fansite is to be believed, then it's Tommy Six
declaring his love for the song and the entire project.[1]

---

1   Tommy Six had a connection with Onej Tuocs that
became clear during the recording of 'But Now the Fox'.
That giddy yelp is Six's uncontrolled excitement at feeling
conected to the band again, musically.

I saw a film once with Matthew Perry where he played this guy who smokes weed one night and ends up with depersonalisation disorder.[2] The weed did it. It threw me off for a while because I've never tried drugs, between the night terrors and depersonalisation I always felt I didn't need an extra hit of surrealism. But Matthew Perry was just a normal guy who developed DPD because of drugs, and that's a real shitty way to look at a mental disorder.[3] I think my Depersonalisation Disorder came about from a lifetime of failing to acknowledge or deal with recurrent abuses. I stayed with Marley for 7 years even though she was awful and violent and mentally abusive. I bottled up the sexual assault I suffered in the military. I just refused to come to terms with any of these things, instead choosing to let them simmer in a mind that wasn't prepared to turn the heat off.

---

2   The film is 'Numb'
3   Turns out the guy who wrote the film has DPD, so maybe smoking weed at the wrong time might change some mental faculties and distort reality in a permanent state.

Animal, Vegetable

31/05/2021

Roisin Dunnett

I am no longer baby I want power

Part 1

'I'm Baby' was the best meme she had ever seen. Unqualified, forever: none would ever surpass it. Other things she saw on the internet, things that made her laugh or feel happy or recognised or guilty or despairing (for these were really the emperors, the fear, the lust and the rapture of the church of memes), none of them came close to matching what she felt when she beheld I'm Baby.

She experienced something that was akin to joy. The joy of recognition, such as a lover could provide. A sense of peace, like looking at an image of God: the truth, but also being told what to do.

How could she explain something like this to her parents? By the time they had grasped its meaning, all the concepts that formed the foundation of the image, it would have disappeared. They did not even know what a Kirby was. *She* barely knew it was a Kirby, in fact had mistaken it initially for a Jigglypuff. Now she knew it was a Kirby, however, it seemed impossible that it should be a Jigglypuff. That it should be a Jigglypuff would render it a lesser thing.

Her parents could not be expected to understand any of this, so she did not tell them.

To claim 'I'm Baby' was to to recognise your helplessness. Kirby, smiling with his pointer, recognised it in himself. But Kirby's announcement did not sadden him. In fact, with that little presentation on a pull-down screen, he appeared less to be announcing than teaching, instructing: *can everyone see in the back? I'm Baby.*

From a spiritual perspective, as far as she could tell, it was common and reasonable to proclaim yourself a Lowly Worm, blind and soft and slow moving. But to explain 'I'm Baby' was to crave some leniency. *How can I,* one could say, *when I'm Baby?* Like a child of god, but moreso. Sure, you could reprimand a child, teach it the rules. What could you do with a Baby?

She was on the way to a friend's house one night, late, drunk. Actually she thought that she might be a bit too late, so she walked quickly, with a bottle of wine under her arm. In front of her was a fashionable woman, a little younger than her. She admired how her hair was: all the way down past her waist. The fashionable woman had buffalo style trainers on, no socks. As she watched, the woman's Achilles tendons strained in the sick orange street light, in the blue and red lights of the chicken shop's illuminated chicken head. She was just trying so hard: so hard to get these gorgeous, major, shoes off the ground. It was admirable. But not necessary, all that strain. Not for one who was Baby.

The picture that went with, or was, or represented, 'I'm Baby' was set against a background of a blue floor and walls. You could only see a little of the blue, which framed the central image. They implied a corporate setting for the scenario unfolding. The scenario, the scene, was of Kirby standing beside a plain white screen. On the screen it said:

i'm baby

Kirby indicated the words with a plain white stick. Kirby had his eyes closed, smiling mouth open, like he was sermonising about the Good News. She had set the image as her wallpaper and her screensaver. She looked at it on the way home from her friend's house, much drunker by then. She switched to a video of a cat playing the flute. Then back to 'I'm Baby.' She was so drunk she nearly fell asleep, jerking up only when the phone finally slid out of her hands and onto the floor of the bus.

The next day she was very hungover, and one thing she noticed was that the sink in the bathroom of her flat was filthy. She got out the chlorine smelling surface cleaner. As she scrubbed the pale yellow crust on the sink she thought: *I shouldn't be doing this*. Was she not Baby?

Another time their kitchen was invaded with ants, attracted to the rotting, creamy effluence on neglected piles of crockery. The ants had it together: they formed neat and intersecting lines, carried each according to its strength. Her flatmates demanded something be done about the ants, and she did not disagree, but what could she do? After all, she was Baby.

There was a man she was seeing who she had been

intending to break up with. In fact, he called her *baby*. But he was mean and overbearing and she was dreading telling him she no longer wanted to see him. When she realised she was Baby, it occurred to her that she need not break up with him. How could she? Instead she became listless in his presence, and often fell asleep while they were together. She acquiesced to his desires, but showed no reciprocal interest. When he said something that made her want to cry, she let herself, not explaining what was upsetting her because it was too hard. She would just say that: 'I *can't!* Its too *hard!'* Eventually, though he was too possessive to break up with her, he left her alone, because she was fucking impossible to deal with.

She went to synagogue for the first time in forever to watch her second youngest cousin get Bar Mitzvah'd. Her aunt invited her to dress the Torah during the service, assuring her that it would be easy: it was not. She fumbled desperately with the ribbons and jingling caps of this most holy of texts for what felt like hours, and then shook a bunch of hands and retreated to her seat. When her youngest cousin's turn came, she tried to refuse, but somehow was tricked into participating again. She stayed awake most of the night before thinking about it, imagining fucking the task up in her stiff green dress, in front of everyone and specifically her grandmother. When, at the appointed time, she was invited to stand beside the pulpit, in the alcove where the Torah rested, she did so. But, though the kind elderly lady in a smart purple jacket motioned with her hands, her own hands remained useless by her sides, until the woman herself dressed the Torah. She went to sit beside her parents, who did not seem to have noticed. In fact, no one noticed that she had not done what she was asked. Her aunt thanked her very graciously afterwards as, after some prompting, did her cousin, who looked proud but profoundly fatigued, near collapse. It was shocking to see her, with that corpse like pallor, running between the adults to meet her friends, little frizzy heads, by the marble cake. Her cousin was a wonderful pianist, showing, apparently, great promise for someone of her age.

Kirby was a candyfloss pink videogame character, who came from the country of Dreamland, on planet Pop Star. Kirby was soft and flexible, could inflate or flatten, bounce high in the air. Kirby's principal method of battle was the absorption of an enemy's powers – Kirby would become engorged, like a puffa fish, by their acts of violence, only to vomit the violence, unchanged, back out at them again. Kirby was not a breaker, but a bender. Kirby had an optimistic personality.

Since adopting the doctrine of 'I'm Baby', she slept whenever she wanted to. If she was tired during the day she found somewhere to lie down and go to sleep. She let bills and rubbish pile up around her, and friends eventually came to her aid saying *Are you ok? I think you should think about talking to someone?* Some of the ones who had been through something similar, or what they thought was similar, said things like: *Look I'm going to come round and tidy your room, and then we're going to go through some of these bills together.* Some of the ones who were doing quite well said *What are your bank account details?* People cooked for her and took her along with them to parties and gatherings, and no one seemed to mind that she stood listlessly against walls, staring into space.

Some people in fact seemed really to like it, people were attracted by her listlessness. She exuded a void-like charisma and fucked extravagantly during that time, people who, in their turn, became drawn into the orbital clusters of people who did things for her, carried her around, met each other for coffee to speak of her in hushed and loving tones. She never paid for anything any more, not drinks or meals out or even most of her groceries. How long would people put up with this?

She did not lose her job in the cinema, but the cinema paid badly and required little of her. It was known to be a bottleneck for lost souls. No one commented if they happened to find her asleep on the floor of the staffroom under a coat: this was normal at the cinema, if the sofa was taken. When she was assigned to tearing tickets she would sometimes watch the films, many of which she had seen before, and close her eyes, registering only flashes of light and darkness as the projections illuminated her face.

She went to a talk by an artist she admired. The artist was witty, and full of an electric energy. Despite this energy, despite the artist's position (a position which involved mature activities, such as speaking confidently of her work to a room full of other adults who clapped politely and drank alcohol from glasses) despite all this she felt the artist understood something about the business of being Baby.

In response to one question the artist had replied with a long, deep sigh before saying: *Left to our own devices, we always strive for happiness. But that isn't always what we're supposed to do with our lives.*

She surfaced, briefly – was that what she had stopped doing? Striving for happiness? So what, then, was she supposed to be doing with her life? The artist had not indicated whether one should strive for something else, instead.

At the flat they got in trouble for letting a tree grow through their fence. The tree's victory over the landlord was satisfying to her, and she wasn't bothered when someone came and chopped it back – it would regrow. She didn't keep houseplants, and those that found their way into the flat invariably died of neglect, but she had begun to admire the universe of vegetation from afar: it seemed to be the only type of visible organism with true allegiance to itself, that could be neither bullied nor fooled. Increasingly she noticed the slyness of plants, gobbling up the poison in the sky, pushing roots into brick and chain link. Even being eaten was a part of their grand plan. Their patience was unbearable, their language incomprehensible. Their resistance was limitless. They seemed to hold no grudges.

She felt no kinship with the plants – their passive nature, if passive it was, bore no relation to the human state of being a baby. She couldn't feed off the sun, and was not patient but somnambulant. The new, slow pace of her life had, however, moved her closer to their frequency, and the lives of plants accordingly became more vivid. She took slow, drowsy walks, and looked at trees on the sides of the road, at weeds growing between paving stones. Window boxes, bursting with these mute, mysterious life forms. Her walks stretched out, taking her through parks, onto marshlands. She would squat down and examine the plant life, their sexual organs, obvious and mystifying, pulling their flowers apart in her fingers. They had no eyes, but they knew she was there. She knew they were more powerful than her and all her kind, and this knowledge reassured her. She liked weeds the best.

Sad Boy Aesthetics

30/06/2021

Alex Mazey

PROLOGUE

Towards the Genealogy of
a Sad Boy Aesthetics

(ɔ◕‿◕)ɔ

One lonely summer, years after they'd electrocuted the Rosenbergs, and my consciousness had been born unfairly into existence (very edgy), a boy was writing his first ever shitpost; a creepypasta about the video game 'Stardew Valley' – I'll spare you the details.

At the beginning of a 1981 philosophical treatise, 'Simulacra and Simulations', Jean Baudrillard writes: 'The simulacrum is never that which conceals the truth--it is the truth which conceals that there is none. The simulacrum is true.' In a meme once observed, late at night, a mysterious non-entity that may or may not exist had replaced the word 'simulacrum' with the term 'shitpost'. 'The shitpost is never that which conceals the truth--it is the truth which conceals that there is none...'

According to the Wiktionary definition: 'shitpost (plural shitposts) (Internet, slang, vulgar, derogatory) A worthless post on a messageboard, newsgroup, or other online discussion platform.' The interchangeability of these terms, simulacrum and shitpost, refers to a coalescence in meaning, I think. That a shitpost, in many ways, doesn't conceal the truth regarding a regular, non-shitpost, but rather conceals the fact that all posts are shitposts.

In many ways, all books are very longwinded shitposts too; especially a book on the genealogy of sad boy aesthetics, which will explore, in more ways than one, the complex aesthetics of Gustav Åhr – better known as Lil Peep – an American rapper, singer, songwriter and model who lived for a short twenty-one years, between November 1, 1996 and November 15, 2017.

Lil Peep 'began making music in his bedroom,' writes David Peisner of 'Rolling Stones Magazine', 'using a MacBook outfitted with GarageBand and a microphone he bought at Guitar Center.' Despite the buzz of an online following that emerged in the earlier years of his SoundCloud success, Gus ended up on the trash heaps of Skid Row, staying in a crowded loft; a dream factory of rappers and producers out to make it big in LA. This was long before his $6,000-a-month stipend provided by First Access Entertainment.

On Skid Row 'he connected with Lil Tracy, Fish Narc and Coldhart,' Peisner continues 'all members of the emo-rap collective Gothboiclique (GBC).' I would be introduced to the conception of such a collective a few months after my foray into creepypasta, when I would first listen to the track 'benz truck (гелик)', and hear the computerised, virtual voice of a feminine entity call out the name, eerily so, 'Gothboiclique'.

'SoundCloud rap is only a few years old,' Peisner concludes, beginning the culmination of an interview with Liza Womack, Gus's mother and producer of the Lil Peep documentary, 'Everybody's Everything'. 'But the careers of three of its most prominent stars — XXXTentacion, Tekashi 6ix9ine and Peep — have ended disastrously.'

It would be easy to write another book about disaster, but this book isn't about disaster since disaster would suggest something has changed in a landscape of the real – rather than diminished. Lil Peep's lifework embodies a mode of disappearance, which makes the aesthetics presented in his lyrics and creative output worthy of an interrogation.

Even in death, Lil Peep reveals something.

'Look,' Womack tells 'Rolling Stones Magazine', 'We think American capitalism is a horrible thing.'

It is no coincidence that Gustav Åhr passed, aged twenty-one, in close proximity to the Sonoran Desert, which embodies, I think, the desert of America itself. This book is a shitpost concerned only with the aesthetics of that Baudrillardian desert from which we will all be commanded to live; an aesthetics of the melancholy.

'We will live in this world,' Baudrillard writes, 'which for us has all the disquieting strangeness of the desert and of the simulacrum, with all the veracity of living phantoms, of wandering and simulating animals that capital, that the death of capital has made of us—because the desert of cities is equal to the desert of sand—the jungle of signs is equal to that of the forests—the vertigo of simulacra is equal to that of nature—only the vertiginous seduction of a dying system remains, in which work buries work, in which value buries value—leaving a virgin, sacred space without pathways, continuous as Bataille wished it, where only the wind lifts the sand, where only the wind watches over the sand.'

(っ◔◡◔)っ

'By now, very little a few haunting refrains lingering at

the back of your mind separates you from the desert of the real.' On page sixty-two of 'Ghosts of my Life', Mark Fisher referred to 'The male lust for death' prevalent within the surface operations of rock music, having existed long before Ian Curtis intoned his trans-melancholic considerations onto the iconography of a loaded gun.

Fisher was careful to give a genre-specific account on the signs and associations of the death drive as occurring within the pernicious surface-dwelling of rock music, smuggled into the genre by way of 'libidinous pretexts'. Over one-hundred pages later, it seems Fisher projected a similar theory onto the more contemporary manifestations of Drake and Kanye West, who were both 'morbidly fixated on exploring the miserable hollowness at the core of super-affluent hedonism' from which Fisher suggests, albeit sub-textually, I claim, that the consumerist death drive of capitalist realism exists, perhaps, at a pancultural altitude.

Prior to this analysis of mainstream hip-hop, Mark Fisher wrote that 'A secret sadness lurks behind the 21st century's forced smile.' An analysis that seems to run parallel to the Baudrillardian analysis of contemporary fascinations – the smile of Tom Cruise, a given example, existing only as a means of simulation.

'Smile and others will smile back.' Baudrillard writes, 'Smile to show how transparent, how candid you are. Smile if you have nothing to say. Most of all, do not hide the fact you have nothing to say nor your total indifference to others. Let this emptiness, this profound indifference shine out spontaneously in your smile.'

In the cybography of Lil Peep, one of the natural predecessors of hip-hop's 'registered melancholy', the 21st century's forced smile had been dropped to reveal a sadness that was no longer secret but could now exist at the level of collective disclosure. Alternatively, Mark Fisher's analysis of rock music's death drive symbolism could adequately explain why Lil Peep's earliest music, posted to SoundCloud, as previously mentioned, was tagged as '#Alternative Rock', a situation that left many music journalists characteristically disorientated at the time.

The difficulty with Lil Peep's categorisation and analysis can be located in how Gustav Åhr was an artist who was dead serious in a time when irony, in the phrasing of David Foster

Wallace, 'tyrannises us' becoming 'the song of a bird that has come to love its cage.' In Lil Peep's mallgoth sincerity, 'I wanna die too / we all wanna die too', the ontologies of a suicidal culture become accelerated, no longer concealed, but made real. Suicide, according to Fisher, had 'the power to transfigure life, with all its quotidian mess, its conflicts, its ambivalences, its disappointments, its unfinished business, its waste and fever and heat – into a cold myth...' It could be said that the seriousness of Lil Peep's confessionalism, in hindsight, only became solidified in his death, since 'Suicide was a guarantee of authenticity,' as Mark Fisher states, 'the most convincing of signs that you were 4 Real.'

If we are all melancholic, as Baudrillard writes, then what comes after melancholy? Suicide? Overdose?

In many ways, the only way for Capitalist (Hyper)Realism to become real – to thoroughly mythologise itself as the only system left to us – so to speak – it must die spectacularly in the simulation of its death; another guarantee of authenticity, to disappear when it still has more to say, to embody its mode of disappearance – to haunt us. As such, the praxis of late capitalism accelerates towards this thirst for annihilation from which it can affirm a mythological status.

'When I die, you'll love me...'

In Baudrillard's 'Forget Foucault', Sylvere Lotringer provides a fascinating insight; 'Traditional societies had no history, but they had a mythology; we're discovering now that history may have been our mythology.'

Without the mythologies of history as an operative referent – mythologies that find themselves increasingly attacked as systems of construction and belief, namely constructions of the powerful, capitalism looks towards its death for justification. The performative credibility of late capitalism's death drive is what Ted Kaczynski might have called a neat trick of the system, since, as Baudrillard responds to Lotringer, 'credibility alone is what gives things meaning,' the element that keeps us 'trapped in the imaginary.'

(ɔ◕◡◕)ɔ

Viewed from this Baudrillardian perspective, it seems a person trapped inside the realms and operative workings of the imaginary can only begin to disintegrate. Here, we observe the deterrence of the actual by way of the virtual. Speaking with Gus' older brother, David Peisner writes how Oskar Åhr 'believed that the Xanax-popping, death-obsessed lothario of Peep's songs was merely a persona. Peep himself would draw that distinction,' Peisner concludes, 'later telling a friend that "Lil Peep is not well, but Gus is fine."' Nevertheless, Oskar admits, 'Over time, the line between the two seemed to disappear.'

Pothos

31/07/2021

Rosa Campbell

You must begin. You must pick a point in time — *before, after* — & simply go from there.

(Everything now is either *before* or *after*.)

Sliding down the dark wood spine between Literary Criticism and Poetry (Anthologies), I sit on the floor of Edinburgh Central Library & get weepy about my dead dad.

It has been almost a year since he died & I am plagued with the feeling that I've done it all wrong — the grief thing. I have refused to read the many books & articles sent by my endlessly kind-hearted friends, I have had no noticeable "stages." On the couple of occasions I've called my mother in tears, she has seemed, frankly, relieved.

I am aware, at least superficially, that there is no right way to grieve, yet this paradigm also seems highly suspect. There are definitely wrong ways to grieve — the ways that make people assholes to those trying to help, the ways that turn you cold, the ways that include self-harm, self-sabotage. Grief can make people vigilantes, it can make them weak, self-centred, self-indulgent. It can make them lash out, panic, career their bikes into pedestrians, dress like idiots. It can make them wild-eyed furies or it can make them wet blanket hermits. It can, most commonly and most egregiously, make them boring.

What a dull, mundane fucking thing it is to be sad about death.

Before the library & the weeping I was in a cemetery, sitting on the tombstone of Jane Lady Lees (d. 17 May 1853) whilst my partner — gently exasperated & resignedly amused — tells me off for being disrespectful. His name is Moss & we are in love. Idiotically, life-ruiningly, giddily in love. In a week we will be 400 miles apart for a while & I will be back to sleeping with my headphones in my ears & sending him photographs of me brushing my teeth. In just under three years we will be rearranging the living room, working out for the second year in a row how to fit a Christmas tree in a tenement flat. In an hour I will be crying silently in the stacks. For now, however, the sun is out & I am trying to get him to kiss me on top of Lady Lees by telling him about Mary Shelley & Percy fucking on her mother's grave. He is googling & saying *allegedly* a lot.

(I think it is perhaps not particularly profound to connect time(s) like this. Proust did it first & did it perfectly well, no need to pick a moment & move around it as if no one has considered the horror of transience before.)

(And yet—
In ten days he will have heard that his friend has died in a climbing accident in Switzerland, & I will be picturing her boyfriend with whom she has been doing long-distance to California & sobbing on FaceTime whilst Moss tells me that it's okay, that he doesn't do that kind of climbing, that he would never leave me. The way I have managed to make it about me is almost shocking; an indication of the kind of grotesquerie I have allowed myself to indulge in just because I lost someone. My compassion has shrivelled & the cycle of grief is unrelenting.)

In the library, I pull books off the shelves almost at random, sliding out something dark green that declares contemporary literature began in 1990. This makes abundant sense to me, as it is also the year I (*tremulous, wavering, lyric "I"*) began. Brought into the world at Leeds General Infirmary on a Wednesday afternoon (weather: Sagittarius sun, Scorpio moon, Gemini rising) by Janie and Mike — as I would call them for the first five years of my life, until I received a sister and they were suddenly transmogrified into *Mummy* and *Daddy*.

December the 12th 1990: I remember my dad claiming that they had timed it so I never had to live under a Thatcher government. I think now, occasionally, about the astonishing number of Tory governments he has not lived under in the past three years.

In the cemetery and the library, though, it has only been about ten months.

POTHOS (disambiguation)

Pothos may refer to:

- **Pothos** (mythology), a character in Greek mythology
- **Pothos** (plant), a genus of plants
  - *Epipremnum aureum*, a plant often grown indoors (formerly grouped within the genus *Pothos* and commonly known as "pothos")
- A statue by **Scopas**

See also:

- **Pathos**

I am on the number 7, or 14, or possibly 49, trundling interminably slowly up Leith Walk, across the Bridges, up towards Nicholson Street and the National Museum, in whose cavernous whiteness sit three people at a meeting that I am late for. I am on the phone to Éadaoín, because I had a date last night and there is Gossip.

and then

I am walking up Chambers Street, telling Éadaoín I have to go, and seeing — as I walk into the misjudged ground-level-of-a-multi-story-car-park-style entrance to the museum — that I've missed a call from my mother. But I'm late and rushing and it can wait.

and then

I am in the balcony café, the clattering of crockery bouncing off the vault, as the business of the meeting (the literary journal that Patrick and I run under the auspices of the university) is pleasantly derailed by Oli's young son, asleep and then awake in his baby carrier.

and then

I am reflexively checking my phone as P says, 'Lunch? Union of Genius? Soup?' & I am saying 'Ah, just give me a sec, I need to call my mum back.'

and then

I am sat at that table, making that phone call, but in the memory I am hovering in the centre of the Grand Gallery, suspended like dinosaur bones for children to stare up at and through.

And then there is a taxi ride & a train journey & a revolving door & my mother's face & a lift with a family looking at us curiously — me with my big pink & purple hiking backpack, my mother's drained face — & a room & a nurse & *twenty minutes ago.*

Otherworlds:
Essays & Letters on Nature & Magic

31/08/2021

Zoë Brigley & Kristian Evans

Otherworlds

Zoë Brigley
c/w miscarriage

IN the winter before the COVID-19 pandemic takes hold in the U.S., my children and I take a trip to an abandoned shopping mall. Run-down malls have a symbolic significance in America: a legacy of the 2000s and the terrible recession that many places have never really shaken. In *Gone Girl,* Gillian Flynn, describes a bankrupt mall in mythical terms as "two million square feet of echo." In the novel, the empty mall is left to criminals and the poor, but here I am driving under the cracked mall signage, entering a nondescript and beat-up storefront with my two small kids.

We come to see a phenomenon called Otherworld, a "32,000 square foot immersive art installation" in Columbus. The blurb on the website promises "Mysteries unfold as you explore over 40 rooms filled with large-scale interactive art, mixed reality playgrounds and secret passageways. It's an all new kind of art experience where visitors are encouraged to freely explore and interact with a surreal world of science fiction and fantasy."

The day I visit with my kids, I have a hard time getting the eldest inside. The entrance is a David Lynch style corridor hung with red velvet curtains. But once in, the children soon get into the spirit of things. They climb into a huge red mouth, burrow into the belly of a hairy monster, and find inside it a beating heart. There is a room with mirrors where we are refracted and reflected a hundred times, a room where opening a coffin turns the light from sepia to technicolor, a room like a mad scientist's laboratory. We fly through the corridors, the twists and turns, test the limits of the 32,000 feet.

But while the children play, something bothers me. In one room, a plastic tree unfurls at the center. In another, stars glimmer on the ceiling, while in another fish are projected on the walls. These are the rooms I like the least. What are we seeking in these human-made replicas?

The children seem dissatisfied now. "Is that all there is?" asks the youngest, as we take a turn through the rooms for the third time. Whatever pleasures there are in lights, colour, and mirrors, there is something superficial about it all, and I can't help thinking of the site's former use: probably a department store in its prime, jewel of American consumerism and high capitalism. But what is it that we are being sold here with all this spectacle?

When my ex-husband picks us up in the litter-strewn lot of the empty mall, he asks me how it went, and tell him that it was amazing, magical, fun. What I don't mention is a nagging feeling. What I don't say is that something about Otherworld is ultimately unsatisfying.

Fast forward to spring, and we are in lockdown in Ohio. I read the news anxiously about potential social distancing and my family in the UK. I lie awake at night thinking about older relatives at risk back in Wales. I am relieved when the lockdown comes to the UK too. In the US and UK we are forced to stay in our homes, only leaving for trips to the supermarket or daily exercise in the local area.

But when the lockdown comes, when social worlds are closed to us, something strange happens. The British newspapers print photographs of queues of cars in the Snowdonia National Park, and U.K. beaches are bustling despite the lockdown. The first weekend of the lockdown here in Ohio, we drive to a local lake that is normally a quiet spot, but we turn back from the main carpark because the lot is overflowing with cars. Further down the lakeshore, we find a quiet place to park. At the lakeside, a group of people gather, despite the warnings, to be baptized. A white man in a baseball cap lowers them one by one into the murky water, shouting: "In the name of the father and the son and the holy ghost." Through his binoculars, our eldest kid watches crowds of people walking across the dam to see the views.

What is this logic? How strange that the first instinct of many is to visit spectacular sites of nature or holiday spots despite the warnings about social distancing. I remember the visitors to Otherworld, charging around the dark interior, demanding to be entertained, circling around the same rooms over and over again. Are we making nature our immersive experience now that places like Otherworld are off-limits?

Now the circle closes. To flatten the curve, we stay in our local area, on our daily exercise forced to examine unspectacular paths and everyday hedges. But is there something we could find there, something more nourishing and less superficial?

The ancient Celts believed in an Otherworld. In Welsh and Irish myth, the Otherworld existed beside our own, on the edge of where we were living, and on occasion intruding or inviting visitors in. The hero would find a ball of silver thread rolling away into a mist that would be a portal to a world that was not our own but filled with the things that we like to forget or ignore.

In the shutdown, I am caught in the circle of my own neighborhood, but it is not for the first time. This time last year, I was grieving a late and terrible miscarriage. I saw no one, went no further than my house if I could help it, but I found myself walking the railroad tracks a few streets away from my house. I would wander through the woods, and at first, I found nothing remarkable. That spring, branches moved faintly in the wind, and the white and purple hepatica flowers pushed daintily through leaf litter under the trees.

But maybe the ball of twine left for us follow is the edge of a real Otherworld, because we have seldom as a culture appreciated the eeriness and beauty of nature in its most mundane and unspectacular forms. When I was grieving and walking in the scrubby woods last year, I felt a sudden relief when a thought struck me that even here, everything was animated and lit with eerie beauty.

There is nothing good about COVID-19, nothing that can make up for the deaths, the illness, the institutional blunders and mis-steps, the losses, but if we must endure it, perhaps there is something we can admit. As we try to survive physically and mentally in lockdown, we are being forced to pay attention. We are being asked to look at how we are living. We are stepping out of the spectacle of capitalism, and although we treat the earth and nature with routine contempt, the world does not revolve around human beings. It never did. There is an Otherworld beyond humans, and it is awake. It has always been awake.

Dance!
The Statue Has Fallen!
Now His Head is Beneath Our Feet

30/09/2021

Richard Capener

The stories Bristol tells itself are written all over. On Gloucester Road, someone's graffitied INJUSTICE ANYWHERE IS A THREAT in white bubble font.

Clapping in 4/4.

Rave horns and cheers.

A thump.

Clapping in 4/4.

Rave horns and cheers.

When I was a housecleaner, my boss parked on a quiet street between jobs. I sat in the car eating my lunch as she bought hers. A woman walked while a car drove around the corner and slowed. A man in the passenger seat, no older than 30, rolled down his window and shouted, 'You fucking freak.' My boss came out of the newsagent as it happened. She got into the car and said, 'They're taking the piss out of him because he wants to be a girl.'

23:31

22:13

21:33

21:18

21:08

20:45

20:36

20:18

20:15

20:04

20:01

After redundancy from housecleaning, I temped at a warehouse in Avonmouth. The job involved unloading lorries, on arrival from manufacturers, and then loading lorries for home deliveries. There were four of us including the boss, Ginge. The team kept asking me, 'Do you know any jokes? Do you know any at all? C'mon! You must know some!' What they meant was, 'Say something racist! Our humour's predicated on reinforcing our identity! This is how we enact our hatred of the other!' A few months after I began, a twenty year old from a Chinese family joined. The team treated him like an equal. One afternoon, we were waiting at the bay for a lorry to arrive. Ginge kept asking him, 'Do you know any jokes? Do you know any?' He shook his head. Ginge began, 'What did the black man say to the Asian?'

Hip-Hop-O-Crit

31/10/2021

Scott Manley Hadley

1. A Rap About Tom Jones, Scott Hadley, & Philanderers

May 13th, 2012

Lyrics:

People say I've lost it cuz I'm losing my hair,[1]
But I'm still badass, I'm still there.
I'm still fucking cool, I'm still fucking dandy,
I'm as popular now as late eighties John Candy.[2]

People say you have to be young to rap[3],
But I don't really want to have to think about that.
Cuz I make my beats at the kitchen table[4],
I mean more business than Vince fucking Cable.[5]

I live for the music, I live for the rhyme[6],
I'm a product, yeah, of my place and time.
I rap about real life and what goes on,
I read the papers, I'm fucking switched on.

Just this morning, for example, in the news
I read about a country that's running short of food.
Don't remember where it was, somewhere below the equator
But I do remember the name of the paper.

The name of the paper.[7]

[pause rapping for a few beats]

---

1   It is apt, I suppose, that even aged 23 with a full(ish) head of glorious, thick, brown hair, I was already fearing for its loss. I had an ever-higher widow's peak from the age of about 17, but I didn't shave my head until three years after this rap was recorded, when 26. The decision to become a rapper was meant to be an aggressive attempt at reasserting my own sense of youth, of potentiality, of *hope*. Even within that, though, I struggled with unfelt posturing and – crucially – opened my rap oeuvre with a line drawing attention to the thing I was most ashamed of: my early onset hair loss.
2   Who was *very* popular. Honestly, though, I wasn't.
3   As I commented above, I was 23 years old when I recorded this, but I felt *too* old, somehow. I still do.
4   100% accurate.
5   At time of rap composition and performance, Vince Cable was a British cabinet minister and member of the House of Commons, during the (now infamous) Conservative-Liberal Democrat coalition of 2010-2015. His job title was Secretary of State for Business, Innovation and Skills, and thus NO ONE in the UK "meant more business" than Vince fucking Cable. Except Hip-Scott, apparently.
6   I do not and I never have.
7   It isn't mentioned, but it would have been the Guardian online.

I come from the Midlands, suburban England,
Let me run through a bit of my personal history.[1]
Born in a small town where not much goes on,
I jumped the county line to Stratford-upon-Avon.[2]

Got my education, it served me well[3],
Learnt about Shakespeare and the Lamp[4] as well.
Did everything I could, my crossdressing[5] glory,
Then I moved to Wales, but that's a different story.

---

1   Getting cocky enough to drop the rhyme and hope no one notices, right in the second verse of my first ever rap. It's a bad look and speaks volumes about the litany of half-cocked verses I was to pen over the following few years.

2   What this means is that I passed the 11-plus and went to my achingly middle class grammar school, just outside of Stratford-upon-Avon, Warwickshire, rather than the comprehensive high school in my own hometown of Redditch, Worcestershire. That famous Worcs/Warks county line that just keeps gettin' "jumped".

3   It didn't. At time of writing these notes (fyi late Summer 2018), I am thirty years old and annotating my own rap lyrics from six years ago while sat in a tiny studio room in one of the most beautiful cities of the world, unable to afford much beyond rent except for Lidl's blesséd €1.79 cava. To be fair to myself, I'm having a great time here in Barcelona, but I don't think there are many people who would consider my adulthood as evidence of my education having "served me well". For those unaware, my adulthood has mostly (so far) been spent as a millionaire's depressed male mistress, but since I lost that job I've been an underemployed dilettante poet slash English-as-a-foreign-language tutor slash dog owner slash occasional copywriter. I've had adventures, yes, but I am not what anyone – except my dog – would call a *success*.

4   What this means is that the previous line may **actually** have been more knowing than I'd presumed, because the Lamplighter (or, as we affectionately called it, "The Lamp") was the pub we used to drink in, underage, in Stratford-upon-Avon. Maybe I'm alluding to my education serving only to teach me how to rely on intoxication to drown my feelings? Maybe not, though: I don't think I was very wise to myself aged 23.

5   I would get back into "crossdressing", i.e. drag, in a big way when a little older. (Note from late Summer 2020: At time of writing *this* note, I identify as non-binary whenever I have the option to do so on a form, but I'm scared to inhabit a non-cis identity publicly because I read so bluntly as "man" to strangers and I fear confrontation over something that matters so much. I'm a very masculinised person (slightly above average height, bald, stocky due to being overweight), though I do frequently wear jumpsuits and patterned clothes, neither of which are standard for "men" here in Toronto, where people dress far more conservatively than in London and Barcelona. Every time I'm asked to provide pronouns in a real-life setting, though, I have a panic attack, which I'm good at doing silently now. I recently bought a lovely, flattering, plain, dress to wear, but it's been wrapped up since I tried it on (and felt spectacular) because I'm too scared of the risk of abuse if I were to wear it outside. I don't feel comfortable in my body, at all, at all, at all, but I don't feel comfortable doing anything to change that feeling, other than regularly doing cardio while watching prestige television shows, which I suppose must be keeping me from being even fatter and even more repulsive to myself. I come from a fat family and I don't want to look like them, it makes me sick to think of doing anything in my life like them. Oh, also, in the interval between writing the majority of the notes here and the scattered few from 2020, I have been diagnosed with Borderline Personality Disorder, which explains a lot and perhaps contributes to my fraught feelings around gender and sexuality, too. For a long time I thought I was bisexual but very, very repressed, and then I thought I *wasn't* bisexual but very, very repressed: I was just heterosexual but ashamed of eroticising female bodies so wished I wasn't; but in hindsight (as an older, wiser, individual), I now think I was right the first time. There's a poem about this in Appendix A.)

Not a fan of rugby so it's kinda hard,
To visit the pubs there without getting barred[6].
So I turned my attention to something even less like home,
And became a huge fucking fan of Sir Tom fucking Jones.[7]

[incompetent guitar solo with mumbled, spoken, criticisms of it]

Born in Pontypridd in 1940,
He's currently a judge on *The Voice* on TV.
His real name is Thomas John Woodward,
He's like a Welsh Elvis but without the big stomach.

He can dance like a bitch[8], he can sing like a god,
He loved the ladies, he shagged around like a dog[9].
Used to play Las Vegas for a month every year,
He's also a boozer, he loves to drink beer.[10]

---

6   This isn't true, because the Welsh are usually very friendly, even the rugby types. (Note from Summer 2020: I remember writing a note here about the normalcy of racism in Wales, but as I didn't spend enough time in Wales *more broadly* to know if Welsh racism was widespread or just a problem with the [vast majority of the] Welsh people *who chose to study in Cardiff,* I deleted it. For example, a woman I knew from the student drama society (yes, I was in the student drama society) had a birthday cake – I'm not making this up – that was "concentration camp" themed. Like, decorated with barbed wire, nails and a miniature "Arbeit Macht Frei" sign. That's pretty fucking extreme racism, I suppose, though knowing one very racist Welsh person and extrapolating outwards about *all* Welsh people is the kinda thing it is churlish to do. I am more than happy, though, to make sweeping judgements about the English as I'm "allowed" to do that and I frequently do both on my blog *TriumphoftheNow.com* and on Twitter, where I can be found and followed at @Scott_Hadley. This generalising about the English happens more than once in the remainder of this text.)
7   The majority of the rest of this song is about Tom Jones, the Welsh pop singer.
8   Uncertain what "a bitch" dances like, and I do not stand by this use of language or imagery in the work of my younger self. But I won't censor it because otherwise how will people understand the *positive* ways society (and Scott Manley Hadley) has changed since May 2012.
9   My dog, Cubby, has no balls (due to deliberate castration, not heart-breaking accident) so I have no personal experience of dealing with horny dogs, except the occasional ones who try and hump my little Tibetan terrier. (Note from Summer 2020: that was a big problem in Barcelona, but wasn't an issue at all in London and hasn't been much of an issue here in Toronto, a city where people have a weird love-hate relationship with dogs that comes from that very North American fear of germs, a societal fear that seemed to evaporate as soon as it became useful. NB: does the cultural germaphobia of settler society in Canada and the USA come from the fact that people here don't forget that bacterial warfare was one of the tools used methodically (both by accident and design) against indigenous peoples as part of the colonisation of the [lands known as the] Americas? People remember that germs can help to commit genocide and are thus hyper cautious? Colonisers forever fearing the retribution in kind from those they displaced/destroyed?)
10   "Beer" is intentionally mispronounced so that it rhymes with "year". Fucking bizarre choice.

A few years ago he stopped dying his hair,
Tom is now a silver fox[1], umm umm yeah[2].
I could go on for hours, spitting rhymes about Tom[3],
But, unlike his wife, I think it's time to move on.

[more competent guitar solo, accompanied by a "dance solo"][4]

See what I mean, I'm rapping about issues,
If I've upset you, here's a box of tissues.[5]
Dry your eyes, get back in the room,
Tom's infidelity doesn't fill the world with gloom.

When he cheats on his wife, it's kinda fine,
Because he's been doing it for years and she doesn't really mind.
She once threw vodka bottles at his head,
And beat him up, so she gives and she gets.

It's not that I'm condoning his terrible behaviour,
You just can't reign in a famous philanderer.[6]

[spoken:] I thought that'd rhyme, I really thought that'd rhyme.[7]

---

1   From a young age, I dreamed of being a silver fox myself. I think it was because, on a deeply subconscious level, I always knew I was destined to be bald.

2   This is, possibly throughout Hip-Scott's entire oeuvre, the laziest rhyming couplet.

3   At no point in my life would this statement have been true.

4   Though I am now terrified by how thin my 2012 *arms* were, I do envy the shape of the lithe body under its clothes. So *boylike*. No, not so boylike: so *androgynous*. (Note from Summer 2020: I remember saying to a friend – and meaning – that I wanted to be so thin you couldn't tell my gender from the side. Now, I would know to use the word "sex" rather than gender there, but the same statement holds true. I hate being bald. I hate being fatter than I used to be, even though I exercise now. I hate my body. It sickens me. I hate looking like a *man*. I hate being addressed as a *man*. I hate hate hate hate myself. Again, see Appendix A.)

5   In the video, there appears a still image of a marketing photograph of a box of tissues, rather than a real-life prop.

6   The six lines preceding this imply a weird and skewed morality where I excuse *both* direct domestic violence and unsanctioned infidelity, by virtue of them cancelling each other out. I was a *young* 23. Now, I am an old, bald, 30.

7   Clearly this "ad lib" serves as a replacement for a couplet that the younger me couldn't be arsed to write.

As for me, I'm nothing like that,[8]
Even when I try to rap I'm no babe magnet.
I've got my books and I've got my coffee,
I'd rather read the Guardian than shag a Miss World hottie.[9]

Maybe I don't have the urge, don't have the eye,
I'd probably rather eat a pizza than stroke a sexy thigh[10].
But bodies like Tom's, they come from the ground,
He's more organic, is the man that shags around.[11]

His urges are animalistic, and so are Tom's songs,
If I did more shagging, could I SING LIKE TOM JONES???[12]

---

8   The song implies, at least in its focus, that a part of me very much *wanted* to be like that.
9   I'd like to be able to call BS on myself here, but I think that at that stage in my life I was very much *scared* of sex, it was something I didn't feel comfortable doing and, as such, avoided aggressively. I am one of the few men I know who has turned down more potential lovers than he has thrusted up. I say "few", I mean only.
10   This is why I no longer have the woefully thin body I'm shaking in the video to this rap: it turns out that pizza *does* taste as good as skinny feels.
11   I wrote my undergraduate dissertation on *Lady Chatterley's Lover* and you can tell you can tell you can tell.
12   No.

BLOOM

30/11/2021

Becky Varley-Winter

White Truck

Song: Ca' the Yowes to the Knowes, cover by Joanna Newsom

I am looking at a dusty white pick–up truck with thick mud on the wheels, the colour of terracotta clay. The mud clusters on the treads in big red clots.

This truck is in the wrong place.

I know every car on this darkening road, and when they come and go. I give them permission to do so. If I looked at my neighbour driving past and said "Stop," his car would make a dull rattling strangled sound, then it would stop.

I only let them come and go because I am so kind.

My hamlet is small and high up, on a single narrow road where the cloud collects over the valley. Some neighbours left long ago, after the mines closed. Their houses are claimed by brambles, and by the red hips of the dog roses.

Now that it is winter, I shelter in my bungalow most of the time. The garden is surrounded by tangled brush that glows like orange fire in the midwinter light. This shades into pine trees, dropping pinecones that creatures gnaw on in hunger or malice, then you see the wide and purple moors. Beneath, the earth is riddled with hidden pits.

The road is bad, which I approve of. The Wi Fi is also bad, I am told. This discourages visitors. "Oh," they exclaim, lost, waving their smooth squat wands in the air like divining rods. "Where's the Wi Fi?"

I do not need the Wi Fi. It is cursed.

If I require supplies, I walk down, into the valley, to the Post Office Shop, moving quickly, keeping upright. I do not stay long.

Opposite my bungalow is the cottage where Peter lives. It is grey stone, with ivy crawling over the step, and the forest crowds darkly behind it. The white truck is now parked outside Peter's house.

It must belong to my enemy.

My enemy works against me and is always changing shape. He can become a cumulus cloud, a spider descending slowly from the ceiling, a gibbous moon, a baby's face. He has taken people I love. When he is invisible, that is when I am afraid. I prefer things to stay where I can see them, and not change.

I am standing before the enemy's truck with anger filling my body. The urge to slash his tyres is granular as sand, flowing into me like the lower chamber of an hourglass, when somebody says, "Hello?"

A man's voice. The enemy, it must be. I keep my eyes on the clogged wheels as his footsteps approach.

"Do you need me to move my pick–up?" he says.

I feel him looking at me.

"That mud's thick, eh?" he says. "There was such a storm when I was driving up last night, I couldn't see. Was afraid I'd get stuck, then I'd be in a right state. Bad reception up here."

I silently count the stones in the mud.

"I've come to see my dad, Peter. You know him? He moved back here a couple of months ago."

I stay silent.

"He's sick, you see. Didn't tell us, wouldn't call the doctor. Stubborn git."

I do not react.

"…Well. I should go back in. Are you okay?" He laughs a small infuriating laugh, and at this I turn, indignant, searching for a retort.

My voice dies out; the enemy is not as I expected. With terrible cunning, he has taken the appearance of Peter's son, who looks much as Peter did in his youth. He wears the mild expression of a sloth. This disguise is meant to touch me at my weakest. Well! He will not trick me. I meet his eyes with silent fury.

"Okay," the enemy says, making a face. He retreats, raising his arms in a surrender gesture, back towards Peter's house.

Peter and I were children together. Once we leaped, shrieking, from Peter's oak tree into the brambles, then crawled out, bloody and smeared in blackberries. His mother called me a bad girl and a bad influence. I remember the small thorns caught in my skin, and the bruises covered in purple stains, like an outward sign of badness inside me.

I return to my bungalow, feeling troubled. I have faced the enemy, yet the white truck is still on the street. Also, Peter is unwell.

It is a long time since I last talked with Peter. I've avoided seeing him. I know that I look changed, though my hair still has black beside the grey, and my eyes are as blue as they were when we were eighteen, when Peter and I walked together into the moors. That day I was tired from crying, as my mother was Not Herself again. We entered a sharp scrub of gorse. The gorse bushes were covered in fevered yellow flowers. We stayed there until dark fell, and the wind rattled dry branches all around us. That night Peter held me with my back curled against his chest, and my breasts cupped in his hands.

I will make Peter a healing broth and deliver it to him even under the eyes of the enemy.

I simmer the broth: Onions, Garlic, Mint, Lemon, Pepper, Salt, Stock, the Flesh of a Chicken. I carry it in the lidded pan slowly carefully through the blue evening to Peter's house.

My enemy opens the door.

"I am here to see Peter," I say.

"Mary," he says. "Dad said he knows you. Come in."

I step warily over the threshold into the porch. The tile behind the doorbell has kept its design, a fountain of purple flowers. This was once the home of Peter's parents. Now it is his. I have not been inside it since I was young, and I am pleased that it has not changed.

I enter the house with dignity.

"What's in the pan?" asks the enemy.

"Broth," I say righteously.

"That's very kind."

"It's for Peter," I say.

The enemy ladles the broth into a blue bowl. I watch to see that he does not poison it, then take it quickly away from him.

"Mary?" Peter calls. I approach with the steaming bowl and place it before him. He smiles at me. "It's been so long. How are you?"

I gesture that the enemy must leave. He meets Peter's eye before retreating. I look at Peter and nod meaningfully. "The enemy is here."

"Is he? I hope I'm not your enemy, Mary."

"No," I say, "but he is very close."

Peter has a half–amused, half–sceptical look which I know well. We have many means of denying the truth. His breathing is laboured.

I lay my hand on his, to show that I will protect him. "Eat," I say. He lifts it to his lips, blows, sips.

"Very nice," he says. "Like your dad used to make, in winter."

"Yes, the same."

"I was sorry when he died. That must have been hard, so soon after your ma had to go to the Priory."

I nod. "It was the enemy's fault."

"This enemy sounds like a fearsome fellow."

"He is," I say.

Peter looks at me sadly. "I'm so sorry I didn't come back up here then, for the funeral. To pay my respects. I didn't think Orla would like it. Me seeing you, you know."

"I did not expect you to come," I say.

My face is hot. A lie. I had expected him.

"It was silly," Peter said. "We broke up anyway. Afterwards it felt too late to say, how sorry I was."

"It's past," I say. "Eat."

He eats as I sit rigidly on the sofa beside him. His ancient cat nuzzles my head.

"I've been looking for you when I was out," Peter says. "I thought you were hiding from me. Were you? I knocked but you wouldn't answer."

I put my hair in front of my face. "I did not look my best."

Peter laughs. "Is that it! Christ, I thought you hated me. Mary, you're my oldest friend. I don't care what you look like."

I let my hair fall back, and he inspects my face. "You always look okay to me. Maybe you could use some sun. I hope you'll stay for a bit?"

"I will stay here tonight," I say. As protection.

"Dad," the enemy says. He's in the doorway. "Is she all right?"

"It's all right, Danny," he says. "She's okay."

The enemy is confusing me. He is not behaving as I expect. He looks humbled, and has brought me tea. Also a biscuit.

Danny.

"Let's see what's on the telly, shall we?" Peter says. He flicks through channels. I hold his other hand and feel the light pulse through his skin. Nothing will take him, not while I keep watch. The cat purrs loudly into the back of my head and the vibration of it spreads outwards, in rings.

Thriftwood

31/12/2021

Alice Wickenden

Introduction.
Those old melodies still sound so good to me / As they melt the years away (The Carpenters, 'Yesterday Once More')

i

Ihaven't slept in a tent in years. Perhaps this isn't that unusual? I'm in my mid-twenties. At this age, once you've grown out of family camping holidays (assuming both that yours was the sort of family who could afford such holidays and that you were raised by the sorts of people who took pleasure in such trips) when would you? Very few of my friends still camp, although the number is slowly trickling back up as we settle down into our own adulthoods, measure out the sticky ghost shapes left by our parents, look for something affordable to do. Find ourselves gasping for fresh air. Then there are festivals, of course, although I'm not sure they count, those drunken, stoned, sticky nights, when the tent acts as mere reprieve rather than the reason for you to be there in the first place. No festival tent is ever *home*.

And anyway, I haven't camped at a festival since 2014. I don't drink much anymore, if at all – especially not spirits – but the last real memory I have of life in a tent is of sitting cross-legged, doing bright and too-sweet shots of bootleg melon liquor bought in some anonymous duty free, eating the remnants of a giant lemon cake for breakfast, washing the stale crumbs down with cider and gin. Everything that weekend was alcohol-tinged and filthy, and Chris and I, who had once been in love with the same girl – although he didn't know, yet, that when she'd left him briefly it had been for me – were getting grimly drunk enough to face the trek back to the train station and then the journey back to London. Those return journeys are memorable mostly for the way we moved from being part of a tattooed and buoyant crowd to wastrels, outsiders: the crowd slowly ebbing out, a collective dispersal.

We drank even more on the final train back but now that we were no longer festival-goers it just felt sordid. Suddenly, we were just two slightly pissed almost-20-year-olds who hadn't washed for days, smelling of smoke and sweat and music. The commuting adults – who might in their past have been us – decisively avoided eye-contact, afraid of whatever we represented. That final trip back, we had left our cheap, broken tent there: a decision I still feel guilty about in terms of the environment and the way it so accurately captures that careless relationship to cheap plastic dispossession that I am only now unlearning, which also seems symbolically poignant. It was, after all, an ending (several endings, as it turned out) as much as an abandonment.

Although my parents did take me and my siblings camping as children, the real reason that I ever camped enough to miss its absence as viscerally as I do now is that I was a Scout. I say that like it's a confession. But it means *something*. Not many people guess, if they didn't know me from eleven to eighteen, and when I tell them they always seem to forget it, are surprised all over again when it comes up: when my muscle memory kicks in and I tie a perfect reef knot, or when I casually talk about having gutted fish. I know why. I live in London now and have never been successful at either exercising or leaving the city; I no longer hike, except for family holidays with relatives who live in the countryside and own dogs and chickens; I read too much, am accumulating literature degrees like clutter. I don't have a garden, of course, having traded outdoor space for the dubious acclamation of a vaguely central city location, and no amount of houseplants can make the urban lifestyle resemble that of someone properly 'outdoorsy'. And then, finally, no matter how close the relationship between literature and the outside world, it still seems to confuse some people that you might cross between the two, or that you might want to – that *I* might want to. God, how I want to.

Anyway, I get cold really easily, and I like the middle-class trappings of my mid-twenties life: cooking with parmesan, going to the theatre, woollen blankets and second-hand cashmere jumpers, too-expensive coffee that's been lingered over. None of these attributes scream Scout. I'm aware of that.

My first ex-boyfriend James, on the other hand, has stayed in Scouts. His dad was a troop leader, and I still remember with an unsettled awe the way his older brother would come back in the university holidays (where he played Ultimate Frisbee, a fact that sums up that family more than anything else could) and immediately throw himself into helping run the Troop. It was in their blood, or perhaps their bones: a sinew-deep connection to the outside. James was never going to leave Scouts – and he hasn't. He still climbs, runs, and wears fleeces: he still does Jailbreak, a 24-hour event where groups of Scouts on foot try to evade their leaders who are on bikes. Except now he's on the other side: he's a climbing instructor, a good and patient man who runs extreme races with his girlfriend – for *fun* – and encourages children to face their fears. When I spoke to him about this project, he told me an anecdote about how he'd helped a girl get to the top of the climbing wall who at the beginning of the session had been too scared to try. At the closing meeting she had said it was her favourite part of the camp, and he had cried with pride. Telling me the story over a poor internet connection, we both welled up; Scouting can be so good, so important, it can do so much. But he was always much more tangibly, obviously part of that world.

I remember, at sixteen, asking him to wear jeans to a party instead of his normal combat trousers. I was embarrassed at the prospect of an obvious intrusion of the coarser life of Scouts into the social one I was constructing alongside it. And I was embarrassed at my own embarrassment. I was just as terrified he'd challenge me – that he'd ask why I was dating him in the first place, if I didn't like his trousers – as I was that he'd forget my request and wear them anyway. He didn't; he wore jeans. The power imbalance in that relationship was tilted in my favour, or at least it was when we were in my domain, my town. Sure, he was a year older – point to him – but I was conventionally pretty; he was nerdier, although I was cleverer; most importantly, probably, he liked me far more than I liked him, and we both knew it.

By now, you might be thinking that I was not a nice person at sixteen, and it might be true.

In that other world, where James and I had met in the first place, he had the edge. He was better with his hands. He was stronger and knew more than me about how to build things, how to be practical, how to *survive*. (This seems like an exaggeration, and I'm always reminded of that *Peep Show* episode where Mark and Jeremy get lost in the Cotswolds: 'Nobody is gonna die, this is Southern England. Nobody dies in Southern England, Jeremy, that just doesn't happen' – but the point is, even if we were never in any real danger, it felt like we could be. Surely one of the main attractions of camping is the way it feels tangential to risk?) One of my favourite memories of the two of us is of a night on camp where a majority of our Unit – 15 of us, at least – decided to sleep outside. We dragged our sleeping bags and ground mats out once the leaders had gone to sleep (or pretended to) and put them around the embers of the fire. The stars were bright. At least, they are in my imagination, but there is no reason why they couldn't have been in real life too; it must have been reasonably warm, clear enough that we could be confident of avoiding rain. Normally, girls and boys aren't allowed in each other's tents – a rule which was to become one of the defining ones of my relationship to Scouting – but suddenly that boundary had disappeared.

James and I usually occupied an uneasily subdued relationship around other people, uncomfortable with displaying any signs of sexuality, or even a particular enjoyment of the other's company. That sort of vulnerability demands a security we didn't have as teenagers, or in our own emotions. That might be unfair on him, actually: I'm sure *he* had that security, that he was acting according to a distance I imposed. I'm sure I was the one who kept him at arm's length when others were around. But not that night, when we drew our sleeping bags up next to each and slept close together. Somehow, being cocooned alongside him was more intimate than being in the same bed. More intimate again because my friend Caz was pressed close to my other side, whilst he was bookended by someone else. (It might have been Morgan – devastatingly attractive, with cheekbones and an obsession with cars, who would go on to DJ in Cambridge and run into me every so often, a reminder that I couldn't quite leave Scouts

452

behind – or Kyle, simultaneously sincere and wry.) We slept like that, pressed together like puppies, under the sky.

At least we slept that way until about 3am when a fox jumped straight into the middle of the huddle. Even now I can't think what it was after. Foxes are rife on sites, and more than one of my friends had at some point had a piece of clothing stolen (there was a particular fox in Thorrington, Essex, with a real fondness for men's trainers and an uncanny ability to sense the weak parts of tents, a renowned menace) but that leap into a huddled pack of teenagers went against everything I knew about the animal. Maybe it was cold enough to risk it, searching for mammalian heat. Or maybe it knew something sacred was happening: a communion of some sort, a promise. Either way, it woke us all up; someone screamed and the spell broke; the cold snapped at us; the leaders couldn't pretend not to know what was going on and had to come out to tell us to get back inside our damn tents *now*. We were all faintly relieved, I think, to avoid the inevitable disappointment of the next morning, when the night had stopped glimmering. James and I peeled apart and went our separate, abashed ways until breakfast, when everyone collectively re-gathered in the mess tent and regaled all those who hadn't joined us with the tale of our night spent under the stars. Basking in the glorious, tepid friction of being slightly in trouble.

The real reason I find it so odd that people no longer associate me with Scouting is that it was *everything* to me. For years it was the heart of my social life, my emotional life, and – yes – overwhelmingly my sexual life as well, stuttering and awkward as that was. It nurtured nestled threads of trauma and friendship that would come to define teenagehood and puberty for me, and that still entangle me now. Scouts is a story I have never told but am always living. People think they know what it means, but they do not, cannot, not unless they lived it too. I have never left it behind.

Contributors

Aaron Kent
is a working-class writer and publisher from Cornwall. Gillian Clarke said, of his poetry, "Every poem is a dizzy word-dazzle" Andrew McMillan called it "Poetry that vibrates on its own frequency" JH Prynne called it "Unicorn Flavoured".

Charlie Baylis
is from Nottingham, England. He is the Editor of Anthropocene and the Chief Editorial Advisor of Broken Sleep Books. His poetry has been nominated twice for the Pushcart Prize and once for the Forward Prize.

Adam J. Sorkin
has translated 65 books of contemporary Romanian literature, including *A Spider's History of Love* by Mircea Cărtărescu; *Lavinia and Her Daughters* by Ioana Ieronim; and *Quarantine Songs* by Carmen Firan and Adrian Sângeorzan.

Adrian B. Earle
is a writer, poet, and media maker from Birmingham. Interested in innovative ways to tell stories and shape language in new poetic forms. His debut collection *We Are Always & Forever Ending* was a 2021 national poetry day selection.

Adrienne Wilkinson
is a writer living in Manchester, UK. She won the George Gissing Prize from the Manchester School of Arts, Language and Cultures. She is interested in the formation of class, desire and health both on the body and in language.

Afric McGlinchey
is a multi-award-winning poet from West Cork, Ireland. Her collections are *The lucky star of hidden things* and *Ghost of the Fisher Cat*, (Salmon Poetry). A surrealist pamphlet, *Invisible Insane* (SurVision) appeared in 2019.

Alex Mazey
won The Roy Fisher Prize, 2018 and was the recipient of a Creative Future Writers' Award, 2019. He is a contributor to the Academic Journal, *Baudrillard Now*, and author of *Living in Disneyland* and *Sad Boy Aesthetics* (both Broken Sleep Books).

Alice Wickenden
is a PhD student, writer, and poet. She has written on teaching and reading rape in the Times Higher Education and the Brixton Review of Books. In her spare time she volunteers for Abortion Support Network.

Alyson Hallett
Alyson Hallett is a prize-winning poet and Hawthornden Fellow whose books include *Toots* (Mariscat Press, 2017), and *Walking Stumbling Limping Falling* (Triarchy Press, 2017) a conversation with walking artist Phil Smith.

Andre Bagoo
Andre Bagoo is a poet and writer and the author of the essay collection, *The Undiscovered Country* (Peepal Tree Press). He lives in Trinidad with his dog Chaplin.

Andreea Iulia Scridon

is a Romanian-American writer and translator. She studied Comparative Literature at King's College London and Creative Writing at the University of Oxford. Her translations include stories by Ion D. Sîrbu and poems by Ion Cristofor.

Annie Katchinska

was born in Moscow in 1990. She won an Eric Gregory Award in 2018. She was a Faber New Poet in 2010 and her second pamphlet *Natto* was published in 2018 by If A Leaf Falls Press. She lives and works in London.

Annie Muir

lives in Glasgow. *New Year's Eve* is her first pamphlet.

Becky Varley-Winter

is the author of *Bloom* (Broken Sleep Books), *Heroines* (V. Press) and *Reading Fragments and Fragmentation in Modernist Literature* (Sussex Academic Press). She teaches, writes and hopes.

Briony Collins

is an Exeter Novel Prize winning writer based in North Wales. Her poetry book, *Blame it on Me*, was released with Broken Sleep Books, who will also be publishing her prose book, *All That Glisters*, in 2022. She is co-editor of Cape Magazine.

Cat Chong

is a poet, publisher, and proud queer crip, whose durational work flails wildly between conceptual and confessional tendencies. They're a graduate of Royal Holloway's Poetic Practice MA and a current PhD student at NTU, Singapore.

Cathleen Allyn Conway

(she/her) is a creative writing PhD student at Goldsmiths, University of London. She is the author of *American Ingénue* (Broken Sleep Books, 2021) and the full-length collection *Bloofer* (Broken Sleep Books, 2023).

David Spittle

is a poet, filmmaker and essayist. Spittle's first poetry collection *All Particles and Waves* (Black Herald, 2020), followed by the pamphlet *B O X* (HVTN, 2018). *Light Glyphs* (Broken Sleep, 2021) followed the BBC premiere of his first film, *Light Noise*.

David Wheatley

was born in Dublin in 1970. His poetry collections include *The President of Planet Earth* (Carcanet, 2017), and he recently coedited, with Ailbhe Darcy, *The Cambridge History of Irish Women's Poetry*. His novel, *Stretto*, appears from CB Editions in 2022.

Day Mattar

is a cheeky queer poet and performer from Liverpool. They are the co-founder of Queer Bodies poetry collective, and facilitate poetry workshops with various art organisations in the UK.

Dominic Leonard

poems, reviews and essays can be found in The Poetry Review, Poetry London, TLS, PN Review, Pain and elsewhere, and in 2019 he received an Eric Gregory Award.

Emma Hammond

Emma Hammond's books include *tunth-sk* (Flipped Eye, 2011), and *The Story of No* (Penned in the Margins, 2015). In addition she has self-published two pamphlets, *softly softly catchy monkey* and *Sleeveless Errand*.

Gregory Leadbetter

is the author of *Maskwork* (2020) and *The Fetch* (2016), both with Nine Arches Press, and the monograph *Coleridge and the Daemonic Imagination* (Palgrave Macmillan, 2011). He is Professor of Poetry at Birmingham City University.

Hannah Copley

is a writer, academic, and editor, with a particular interest in contemporary poetry and life writing. She explores the use of historical records and archival material in poetry and is an editor at Stand magazine.

Jack Warren

is a gardener & environmentalist from Somerset. He holds masters degrees in both Poetics and Applied Ecology. *Rude Mechanical* is his first pamphlet with Broken Sleep Books.

Jaydn DeWald

is the author of *The Rosebud Variations* (Broken Sleep Books, 2021) and *Sheets of Sound* (BSB, 2020). He is Assistant Professor of English and Director of Creative Writing at Piedmont University in Demorest, Georgia, USA.

Jeff Alessandrelli

lives in Portland, Oregon. In addition to his writing work he also directs the non-profit literary record label/book press Fonograf Editions.

Jessica Mookherjee

is the author of three pamphlets and two collections. *Tigress* (Nine Arches) is shortlisted for best 2nd collection, Ledbury Munthe Prize. She has twice been highly commended in the Forward Prize, and is co-editor of Against the Grain Press.

Jon Stone

is a writer, editor and researcher who specialises in hybrid and chimeric works: rough fusions of form and genre. His poems often concern, or embody, the intermeshing of organic and constructed, human and non-human, real and unreal.

Karen Dennison

is the author of three poetry books – *Of Hearts* (Broken Sleep Books, 2021), *The Paper House* (Hedgehog Poetry Press, 2019) and *Counting Rain* (Indigo Dreams, 2012). She is co-editor of, and cover designer for, Against the Grain Poetry Press.

Kat Payne Ware

(she/her) is a queer poet and essayist, and the founding editor of SPOONFEED, an online literary food magazine. Her debut pamphlet, *THE LIVE ALBUM* (Broken Sleep Books) was published in July 2021.

Kristian Evans

writes about ecological philosophies and the ways in which we receive the 'more-than-human'. He has edited Magma Poetry magazine, and the anthology *100 Poems to Save the Earth* (Seren, 2021).

Kristine Ong Muslim

is the author of nine books, including *The Drone Outside* (Eibonvale Press, 2017), and *Black Arcadia* (University of the Philippines Press, 2017). She grew up and continues to live in a rural town in southern Philippines.

Lawrence Schimel

is a bilingual American writer, translator, and anthologist working in many genres, including poetry, fantasy and science fiction, and children's books, whose work frequently deals with gay and lesbian themes, and with Jewish themes.

Leia Butler

likes to experiment with form, language, and sound. Her projects aim to challenge boundaries of poetry and practice and create something which encourages her audience to think

Liam Bates

is a poet from the Black Country, with work shortlisted for prizes by Magma, Bridport and Creative Future. His full-length collection is due summer 2022 with Broken Sleep Books. Liam lives in Cambridge.

Lotte Mitchell Reford

is a Glasgow-based writer. Her work explores art, gender and fucking, amongst other things, and sometimes falls between genres. She has had writing published in places such as Hobart, The Moth, SPAM, and New Writing Scotland

Lucy Harvest Clarke

is the author of *Silveronda* (if pt hen q). Lucy Harvest Clarke's poems merge the surreal into the common place. Using a blend of sprung rhythm and jacked up line endings a subtle erotic poise bobs up into and then out of sight.

Lucy Rose Cunningham

is a poet, and curator and leader for research workshops with students from across School of Fine Art, University of Leeds

Luke Kennard

is a British poet, critic, novelist and lecturer. He won an Eric Gregory Award in 2005 for his first collection *The Solex Brothers*. His most recent collection, *Notes on the Sonnets*, is shortlisted for the 2021 Forward Prize.

Marlon Hacla

is a programmer, writer, and photographer. His first book, *May Mga Dumadaang Anghel sa Parang* (Manila: National Commission for Culture and the Arts, 2010), was published as part of UBOD New Authors Series II.

Martín Rangel

is a writer, interdisciplinary artist and translator. He is the author of the poetry book *Luna Hiena* (Ablucionistas, 2020) and others. Under the pseudonym RVNGEL he performs rap. As MALVIAJE he produces experimental electronic music.

Morag Smith

is a Cornish poet, painter, writer, and performer. In 2018 she won the Shorelines prize in the Cornwall Contemporary Poetry Festival competition. Zen Buddhist practice is at the heart of all her work.

Penelope Shuttle

lives in Cornwall, her most recent full collection, her 13th, is *Lyonesse*, (Bloodaxe, 2021). She enjoys collaborative working, and in September 2021 Broken Sleep published her and Alyson Hallett's pamphlet of sonnets, *Covid/Corvid*.

Peter Scalpello

is a queer poet and sexual health therapist from Glasgow. Their debut pamphlets were published by Broken Sleep Books in 2021. Their first collection will be published by Cipher Press in 2022.

Phil Thomson

Art college graduate and former advertising copywriter, Phil Thomson, spent many years as a senior lecturer in design - and these days, continues to be successfully at one with his parallel worlds of lyric writing and image making.

Razielle Aigen

Her poems and pamphlets have appeared across Canada, the US, and the UK. She is a recipient of a Research and Creation grant from the Canada Council for the Arts. *A Future Perfect* (Talonbooks 2021) is her debut book of poems.

Richard Capener

has had work featured in Sublunary Editions' subscriptions, SPAM Zine, Streetcake, and Beir Bua. He edits The Babel Tower Notice Board, and co-curates the associated Live From Babel Tower reading series.

Richard O'Brien

publications include *A Bloody Mess* (Valley Press, 2015) and *The Dolphin House* (Broken Sleep, 2021). He won an Eric Gregory Award, 2017, and was the Birmingham Poet Laureate 2018-2020.

Roisin Dunnett

has had short stories appear in Ambit, Hotel Hypocrite Reader and elsewhere. Her non-fiction has appeared in Broadly, Tangerine Magazine and Imperica.In 2018 she was awarded funding to attend the Can Serrat Writer's Residency in Spain.

Rosa Campbell

currently lives in Edinburgh, where she is writing a PhD on the women poets of the New York School and is the Managing Editor of The Scores. Her poetry was Commended in the 2019 Ambit Poetry Competition.

Rosanna Hildyard

is from Yorkshire. Her fiction and poetry has recently been published by PERVERSE, Banshee, Under the Radar and Modern Poetry in Translation. Her short story collection, *Slaughter*, was longlisted for the Edge Hill Prize 2021.

Scott Manley Hadley

is a poet and blogger whose work explores physicality, mental illness, and class. Their books include *Bad Boy Poet* (Open Pen, 2018) and *the pleasure of regret* (Broken Sleep, 2020). Scott was 'Highly Commended' in the Forward Prizes for Poetry 2019.

Simon Barraclough

has published and edited several volumes and pamphlets, most recently the long poem *Iarnród Éireann* (Broken Sleep Books, 2021). His debut collection *Los Alamos Mon Amour* (Penned in the Margins) was a Forward Prize finalist in 2008.

SJ Fowler

is a poet, artist and writer. His work has been commissioned by Tate Modern, BBC Radio 3, Somerset House, and Tate Britain amongst others. He has published 9 poetry collections, plus volumes of selected essays and selected collaborations.

Stuart McPherson

is a poet from Leicester. His debut pamphlet *Pale Mnemonic* (Legitimate Snack, 2021) was followed by *Water Bearer* (Broken Sleep Books, 2021). His work explores the relationship between family dysfunction, trauma, and fragile masculinity.

Traian T. Coşovei

Founding member of the "Cenaclul de Luni" literary circle that would set the tone for postmodern Romanian poetry. Coşovei was the recipient of a series of prizes, including the Romanian Academy and the International Nichita Stănescu prizes.

U. G. Világos

is the author of a variety of books, most notably *The Lark Sings Death*, which is considered a vital touchstone of poetry, though is long out of print. U.G. has not been seen in public for two decades.

Yousif M. Qasmiyeh

is Refugee Hosts' Writer-in-Residence, and a doctoral researcher at the University of Oxford whose research examines the archive, time and containment in refugee literature in Arabic and English.

Zoë Brigley

is a Welsh poet, editor of Poetry Wales, and assistant professor in the Department of English of Ohio State University. She is the author of three collections of poetry: *Hand & Skull* (2019), *Conquest* (2012), and *The Secret* (2007).

Anthologies & Contributors

January 31st 2021 — Crossing Lines:
an anthology of immigrant poetry

Yvonne Litschel, Lou Sarabadzic, Amy Evans Bauer, Yvette Siegert, Gustavo Barahona-López, Emma Filtness, Arielle Jasiewicz-Gill, Mizzy Hussain, Judith Kingston, Isabelle Baafi, Iulia David, George Ttoouli, Cristina Lai, Arturo Desimone, Kavita A. Jindal, Zah Rasul, K. S. Moore, Mike Ferguson, Michelle Penn, Taylor Edmonds, Maia Elsner, Nóra Blascsók, Lady Red Ego, L. Kiew, Hasan Bamyani (tr. James Attlee), Vasiliki Katsarou, Andrés N. Ordorica, Meriem Ahmed, Corinna Keefe

May 31st 2021 — Hit Points:
an anthology of video game poetry

Matthew Haigh, Aaron Kent, Luke Thompson, Maria Sledmere, Jessica Mookherjee, Arji Manuelpillai, Dylan Benjamin, Amanda Crum, David Spittle, Sarah Cave, Jon Stone, Oliver Fox, Clarissa Aykroyd, Jake Wild Hall, Maria Picone, Samuel Tongue, Calum Rodger, Emma Filtness, Liam Bates, Scott Manley Hadley, Lydia Unsworth, Mark Ward, Katy Wareham Morris, George Sandifer-Smith, James Roome, Jasmine Dreame Wagner, Louise Goulding, Niall Firth, Paige Elizabeth Wajda, Rhys Owain Williams, James Coghill, Aisha Farr, Logan K. Young, Callan Waldron-Hall, Rachel Burns, Matthew Kinlin, Sam Kendall, Nick Gerrard, Richard Watt, Tim Kiely, Dan Fitt-Palmer, James Knight, Peter Hebden

September 17th 2021 — Snackbox:
Selected Legitimate Snacks

Aaron Kent, Dominic Leonard, Sarah Fletcher, J H Prynne, Wayne Holloway-Smith, Margot Holloway-Smith, Imogen Cassels, Richard O'Brien, Kyle Lovell, Dom Hale, Astra Papachristodoulou, Stuart McPherson, Rishi Dastidar, Maria Sledmere, Mary Anne Clark, Colin Bancroft, Eva Griffin

October 31st 2021 — Poetry Ambassadors

April Egan, Kaycee hill, Eve Wright

LAY OUT YOUR UNREST

Milton Keynes UK
Ingram Content Group UK Ltd.
UKHW010630010823
426134UK00004B/72

9 781915 079954